PUZZLE PIECES OF LIFE

MY STORY OF

RESILIENCE AND REINVENTION

&

HOW YOU CAN ACHIEVE IT TOO

LINDA WILSON

LEGAL DISCLAIMER

This book is a work of autobiographical fiction. While it is inspired by real events and personal experiences, names, places, and identifying details have been changed to protect the privacy of individuals. Any resemblance to actual persons, living or dead, or real businesses is purely coincidental. Certain characters are composites or fictionalized for narrative purposes.

Additionally, the author acknowledges having signed nondisclosure agreements during certain periods of employment. As such, this book does not disclose confidential, proprietary, or sensitive information related to any organization. The experiences and reflections shared are personal and do not represent the policies, operations, or views of any specific company or entity.

PROLOGUE

Puzzle Pieces Of Life is a transformative story, piecing together the author's journey through a series of career changes, each experience becoming an essential part of a larger picture of resilience and self-discovery. Confronted by a string of profound personal tragedies, the author repeatedly rebuilds her life, drawing strength from a range of careers that not only offered stability but also became instrumental in her healing.

In the healthcare field, she learned the value of empathy and human connection during times of suffering. Her business ventures taught her the importance of perseverance and adaptability. Meanwhile, roles in counseling and community service allowed her to guide others through their struggles, deepening her own journey of self-compassion and growth.

Through each career, she encountered new opportunities to reinvent herself, finding solace and meaning in the act of helping others while reclaiming pieces of herself along the way. Woven into this mosaic of loss and career evolution is a story of unexpected romance, a reminder that even in the darkest moments, life can surprise us with love and connection. This story is not just an account of surviving hardship; it is a testament to the power of reinvention and the beauty of embracing puzzle pieces of life, however disparate or challenging they may seem. Readers are invited to walk alongside, learning how they, too, can rebuild, rediscover, and thrive—creating a life rich with resilience, reinvention, and maybe romance.

TABLE OF CONTENTS

DEDICATION

To my beloved husband, for your unwavering love, support, and belief in me through every step.

To the mentors who have guided me for sharing your wisdom and showing me that anything is possible.

And to all those who want to give up—may this story encourage you to take one more chance. To everyone

I have met along this journey with an open mind and an open heart; thank you for your friendship, strength, and unwavering belief.

This book is for you!

CHAPTER 1

THE BEGINNING - FAMILY LEGACY

June 10, 1947, Hello World, is when it all started. That was the day I came into the world with a full head of curly dark hair and a loud, unmistakable cry. At that time, my mother was in the same hospital as her mother, who had fallen seriously ill. Several days later, my mother read in the local newspaper that her mother had passed. It must have been hard for her, balancing the weight of new life with the sudden loss of her mother. I wonder now if she ever let herself grieve or if she buried it all beneath the everyday duties of motherhood.

The song that year was *Linda,* released by Columbia Records. With my grandmother now deceased, my mother named me Linda Louise, adding Louise, my grandmother's first name.

Photo by Linda Wilson

Though my arrival may have been exciting for my parents, I have never been convinced that they genuinely loved each other. My dad was of Irish, Polish, and American Indian descent. He was a diligent worker, much like his father. His father, my grandfather, was a farmer and a game warden, a man who valued demanding work above all else. Naturally, my dad followed in his footsteps, introducing me to the world of crops and livestock early on. Even though Dad never graduated high school, this did not stop him from chasing what he wanted in life.

After getting married, my parents traveled, managing various farmers along the way. Mom attended to the owner's wives. It was in New York that they worked for a very wealthy and childless couple. The wife was enamored with me. She would go shopping with Mom and me and buy me the cutest outfits. Mom was genuinely concerned about this lady's intentions. We soon moved to New Jersey. Mom and Dad realized this was not the lifestyle for the family. We headed back to Connecticut, and Dad went to work as an apprentice to learn machining during the day.

My mother, on the other hand, came from a French and Italian background. She was the youngest of nine children with an age gap of 10 years between her and her sister. As the youngest by a decade, Mom always felt a bit like an only child—often tagging along behind her older siblings, trying to keep up. In 1944, my mom got her first job at the Warner Theater in Torrington, Connecticut. Warner Theater was built in 1931; a movie house described as Connecticut's most beautiful theater. Though the economy struggled nationally, the theater prospered in Torrington, surviving the Depression and a world war.

John Ringling brought the circus to Sarasota and Venice, Florida, for the winters starting in 1927. On Dec. 20, 1959, the Ringling Circus would move from Sarasota to Venice on a site fronting US 41 signing an agreement on leasing 10 to 15 acres for $1,000 a year. The animals would arrive by train, unloaded, and paraded over the bridge to their new home. In 2002, my husband David and I moved to Venice, Florida.

Mom and her sister boarded the train to Hartford, Connecticut, in 1944, where the Greatest Show on Earth, Ringling Bros., and Barnum & Bailey Circus were debuting. When they arrived in Hartford, Mom told her sister that she needed a pair of new shoes for work. Her sister was not thrilled about being late, but she said let us hurry so we do not miss anything. Mom agreed and bought her shoes. As they arrived at the entrance of the circus, they heard loud screaming, saw smoke and fire billowing up from the tents, and people running out of the tents.

Internet photo

The Hartford Circus fire, which took place on July 6, 1944, in Hartford, Connecticut, stands as one of the most devastating fire disasters in U.S. history. The blaze erupted during an afternoon performance of the Ringling Bros. and Barnum & Bailey Circus, which was attended by between 6,000 and 8,000 people. Tragically, the fire claimed 168 lives and left 487 others injured, many of them children. Before the season began in May 1944, the canvas roof of the big top had been treated for waterproofing with a mixture of paraffin and gasoline. The paraffin melted down, mixed with gasoline, and then poured from watering cans and brushed into the canvas. The treatment involved using 6,000 gallons of Texaco white gasoline and 60 barrels of yellow paraffin wax, each weighing 300 pounds, purchased from Standard Oil.

The most well-known victim of the tragedy was a young girl, posthumously referred to as Little *Miss 1565*. Despite numerous attempts over the years, her body remained unclaimed. She was initially buried without a name in Hartford's Northwood Cemetery but was later exhumed and reinterred in Southampton, Mass., in the early 1990s after being tentatively identified as Eleanor Emily Cook. However, this identification is still a subject of debate. On July 6, 2005, a memorial was dedicated at the site of the fire to honor the victims.

Mom never forgot the sound of the screams. She used to say it haunted her how a pair of shoes saved their lives that day. I know that my mom's sister, Mary, was grateful to my mom for insisting that she shopped for shoes before going to the circus. This was only the beginning of tragedies, heartbreaks, and disasters that Mom would experience, shaping my life in ways I could never have imagined.

People always told Mom's parents how talented and outgoing she was. As she walked to school, her smile was contagious, and she often sang her favorite Italian folk songs, her voice ringing out across the neighborhood. Whether she was playing hopscotch on the sidewalk or racing her friends to the end of the block, she brought the whole street to life with her energy. Your Augustina has a voice like a nightingale, Mrs. Rossi would tell her parents with a smile. And she is always so full of life!

Everyone knew her as the social butterfly of the neighborhood, flitting from one group of friends to the next, always leaving lau ghter in her wake.

When she was in high school, she had a once-in-a-lifetime opportunity: a scholarship to the Juilliard School of Music. I imagine her standing there, holding that letter, heart racing with excitement, her dreams just a signature away. But life took a different turn. After their third date, my grandfather told my dad, "Either marry her or move on." She married, and the music was put on hold, her voice silenced by the demands of family and life. I would sometimes hear her humming softly as if she were trying to hold onto that dream.

Dad married my mother, and after a little over a year, I came along. We traveled from Connecticut to New York to New Jersey, as Dad was managing various farms along the way. Mom took care of the owners' wives, and in New York, they met a very wealthy, childless couple. The wife was enamored with me, often taking us on shopping trips and buying me the most adorable outfits.

As I would later learn, my parents argued constantly about the owner's wife's intentions. Mom grew increasingly wary, while Dad, enticed by the generous pay, resisted leaving. Mom said that she remembered the tension in the air and their hushed voices behind closed doors when I asked why she wanted so desperately to leave. Mom had photographs of various complete ensembles that were beautiful and were purchased by the owner's wife.

Soon, they moved back to Connecticut, where Dad started an apprenticeship in machining, eager for stability. This allowed Dad to work a regular day job, and Mom went to work at night selling Avon products in clients' homes. I remember sitting with Dad and listening to The Lone Ranger and The Shadow on the radio. After the broadcast, I would try to wait for Mom to come home. My bed was next to a window, so I would look out that window, gazing at the night sky and biting my headboard, trying to stay awake. All that got me was a chewed-up headboard. While hearing the night's quiet symphony Each morning, I would hear the dairy farmers clinking of bottles delivering milk to our doorstep, the cries of the Rag Man, and later, the cheerful sounds of the Ice Cream truck. Life was simple, you always knew your neighbors, and I do not ever remember locking the doors to our home. There was no need for that in our little community. Neighbors would stop by unannounced, borrowing sugar or eggs as if we were all part of one big household. I remember Mrs. O'Malley, from down the street, would let herself in to check on me if Mom was working late, bringing fresh bread, and chatting with Dad as if she were just another member of the family. It was a different world back then, a world where trust was as common as a knock on the door.

Tides of Change

We were living a modest but contented life when disaster struck. I was nine, and Gary was only two when the historic flood of August 18, 1955, changed everything. For two days, the sky seemed to collapse under the weight of the relentless rain, releasing a deluge of 14.25 inches that drowned our town in despair. The streets turned into raging rivers; the hum of everyday life was drowned by the deafening roar of water. Torrington became a chaotic landscape of floating debris, shattered dreams, and families desperately clinging to whatever hope they could find.

Thousands were left homeless as mom-and-pop businesses were destroyed, roads and bridges were swept away, and even massive factories were reduced to rubble. The flood did not spare anyone, and for us, it took the life of my mother's beloved sister, Mary.

Mary lived in a third-floor apartment in the downtown area, and the water rose so rapidly that she barely had time to react. Without her prosthetic arm, which she could not fasten quickly enough, she clung to the window in desperation. A boat carrying two other women came alongside her, and with great difficulty, she managed to get into the boat. But the rushing waters were too powerful. The boat, fighting against the powerful current, was no match for the bridge's unforgiving structure. As it crashed violently, the women were thrown into the churning waters, their screams swallowed by the relentless torrent. Mary, who had fought so bravely to escape her apartment, was now lost to the same waters that had robbed so many others of their lives and homes.

Internet Photo

Mary's name now stands at the top of the right side of the memorial in Torrington, honoring those who perished that day. As the floodwaters swept away the remnants of our community, rescue crews battled 40-mile-per-hour currents. The relentless waters carried away pieces of our civilization, turning the Naugatuck Valley and every other valley in Western Connecticut into a wasteland of debris. By September 23rd, the bodies of seventy-five people had recovered, with twelve still missing. The statewide industrial damage amounted to more than $114 million. These numbers, reported by the *Waterbury Republican-American*, only begin to capture the devastation. This marked the beginning of years filled with loss and hardship for our family, shaping my life in ways I could never have imagined. Losing our home and everything we owned felt like the ground had been ripped out from under us. The familiar walls that once held our laughter and dreams were now just debris, and all the little things we took for granted, the treasured keepsakes, were swallowed by the floodwaters.

Mom and Dad separated; it felt as if the flood had torn not just through our town but through our family. Dad determined to help others, stayed behind as a volunteer firefighter while Mom, my brother, and I sought refuge at a friend's home. I remember the weight of confusion and sadness hanging over us, the empty space Dad left behind echoing louder than the roar of the floodwaters. Soon, they divorced.

Always a daddy's girl, I would sit on the front steps, watching the road, hoping to see Dad's car pull up. I wanted so badly for us to be a family again, the way I imagined it before the divorce. I would imagine us all laughing together, Mom singing in the kitchen while Dad teased her about her favorite songs. But that dream felt distant, like a fading photograph in an old family album. Still, every other weekend, Mom made sure we got to spend time with Dad. Every Christmas and every other weekend, Dad would pick us up. We would either go to the State Park or go to see our grandparents. She never spoke ill of him, even when I could see the hurt in her eyes. Maybe she was hoping for that dream too, in her own way.

Then along came Bub. He was older, with a weathered face and a gruff voice, but there was something in his eyes that seemed to recognize the silent music in Mom's soul. He was already established in the local music scene with a band of his own, and he rekindled the light in her. When she told us about him teaching her to play the upright bass, there was joy in her voice I had not heard in years. "I'm learning, and I'm pretty good at it!" Mom said, laughing, her eyes shining. But it also meant a shift at home. You will have to do the dishes now, she said one evening, as I am now a member of Ruby's Ramblers, looking at her callused fingers. I cannot have my hands in water; it will soften the calluses I am working so hard to build. I remember standing at the sink, water running over my small hands, feeling the weight of those words. I wanted to be happy for her, but I also felt a sense of resentment. I was just a kid, after all, and suddenly, I had to be a little more grown-up.

Ruby's Ramblers quickly became a hit at the local restaurant and bar, their music filling the small, smoky room every weekend. My brother and I would sometimes tag along, sitting in the corner with our coloring books or playing with the other kids in the back. The room would be buzzing with conversations, the clinking of glasses, and the rich sound of country music. Mom's voice would soar above it all, strong and confident, as if she had never missed a beat. I would watch her on that small stage, her fingers dancing on the bass, her smile wide and radiant. She was finally living a piece of that dream.

My little brother, though just three, was mesmerized by the music. Bub would lift him onto a chair, the giant bass almost swallowing his tiny frame, but he would pluck at the strings with such great determination. I remember the way the room would go silent, all eyes on this little boy standing so proud. The crowd would cheer, and he would beam with pride, his love for music blossoming in those moments. It was a sight that made everyone smile, even me, though I was still coming to terms with our new reality. Years later, his talent would take him far. The same determination I saw in that restaurant carried him through high school, leading his band to win the Battle of the Bands in Connecticut two years in a row. When they got the chance to open for Steppenwolf at Yale University's Woolsey Hall, it was like a dream come true for him. I was already far from Connecticut by then, having left three years earlier, but I still felt a sense of pride—and maybe a little pang of jealousy. He was achieving so much at such a youthful age while I was still finding my way. But in those moments, I knew he was living the dream that had begun with a chair and a bass fiddle in a small restaurant all those years ago.

The relationship between Bub and my mom was getting serious, and we all moved into what today you would call a "tiny house," with two bedrooms, one bathroom, a kitchen, living room separated by a centered staircase. Bub was always good to us, and more importantly, Mom was happy! Bub became a steady presence in our lives, not just as Mom's partner but as a father figure who showed up for us in ways that mattered.

Occasionally, he would take an afternoon off during the summer, and we would all go down to the beach or the local state park. Those days felt magical, the kind where you forget about everything else and just let the sun, sand, and laughter carry you away.

But Bub was also firm when he needed to be. One time, when I spoke back to Mom, he stepped in and disciplined me. I felt a surge of anger and embarrassment; no one other than my mom had ever corrected me like that. I stormed upstairs, heart pounding, and announced that I was leaving. I had seen it in the movies—kids packing their things and leaving when they felt misunderstood. I wanted to make a statement. So, I grabbed a large scarf and stuffed it with as many clothes as it could hold. As I clumsily tied it together and made my way downstairs, Mom was waiting at the bottom. She watched me with a soft smile, almost as if she had been expecting this.

"That looks awkward. Let me help you," she said, her voice calm and steady. I paused, a little taken aback. I had expected pleading or maybe even anger, but not this. She found a long pole and expertly tied the scarf to the end, just like in those cartoons. "This is how you carry it," she explained, then opened the front door wide. "Have a good time," she added, her smile unwavering.

I felt a lump form in my throat as I stepped out, my makeshift bundle slung over my shoulder. I tried to hold on to my defiance, but it wavered with every step down the steep driveway. Halfway down, I stopped and turned around, hoping to see her watching me from the doorway, ready to call me back. But she was not there. For the first time, I felt truly alone. I sat at the bottom of the driveway, my heart heavy, my eyes welling up. The world suddenly seemed so big, and I, so small. I finally got up and started to walk back up the driveway. When I got to the door, she said, "Did you forget something?"

"Yes, Mom," I mumbled, my voice barely a whisper. "I do not think I am ready to go. I am sorry."

She pulled me into a hug, holding me tight. "It's okay," she whispered. "Just remember, you can always go, but you can always come back, too." That day, at the age of nine, I learned to think things through before acting on impulse. And maybe, just maybe, it was the start of my desire to explore the world—because I knew that no matter where I went, I could always come back home.

As the months passed, the little house felt warmer, filled with the anticipation of the holidays. Mom brought out the Advent Calendar, the one she carefully unwrapped each year as if it were the most precious thing. I knew Christmas was approaching, my favorite time of the year.

Despite knowing we were not wealthy, Mom had a way of making it feel like magic was woven into every corner of our home. But that did not dampen her spirit. While we slept, she stayed up late, threading colorful yarn around every piece of furniture, through every doorway, and across the entire living room. When we woke up on Christmas morning, we could not even get out of our rooms without carefully navigating the maze of yarn. Each color was different—one for me and one for my brother, leading us on an adventure through the house. The yarn looped around chairs twisted through the banister, and at times, I had to crawl just to follow it.

Later, we made ornaments for the tree—simple ones. Mom showed us how to fold and cut paper into stars and how to glue lunch bags together, cutting them into three-dimensional shapes. Our tiny house, despite its size, was filled with warmth and love that Christmas. I learned that home is not just about where you live; it is about the people you share it with and the love you pour into it, no matter how little you have.

At the end of the yarn, hidden under the Christmas tree, was a beautifully wrapped present. It was not big or expensive, but it felt like the most special gift in the world. I will never forget that morning, the laughter, the excitement, and how we marveled at Mom's creativity. She taught us that day that it did not take a lot of money to create a lasting memory; you just needed to think outside the box.

Yearning For a Connection

I remember sitting outside for hours after the sun went down and trying to guess the year, make, and model of the cars that would pass by with their headlights on just for something to do.

With few children around to play with, I found myself yearning for connection. That is when I decided to find a pen pal. What began as a single letter blossomed into correspondence with three different pen pals from Hawaii. We exchanged stories about our lives, our communities, and our school experiences, bridging the vast distance between us with each letter. As I read about their island life, I promised myself that one day I would visit Hawaii. That dream became a reality in my late twenties. My girlfriend from Colt Firearms and her husband called, asking if I could house-sit and dog-sit for them while they went on a monthlong vacation to Hawaii. They were preparing to open a Certified Public Accounting office and wanted to take this vacation before diving into their new venture. I happily agreed. As a thank you, they offered me a week's stay in the condominium they had rented as payment for my help. All I needed to do was cover my own transportation to and from Hawaii.

Armed with the old addresses of my pen pals, I wandered the island in search of them, but time had moved on, and they were no longer there. Undeterred, I set off to explore on my own. I discovered that, for just a quarter of a dollar, you could ride a bus that circled the entire island. You could hop on and off as you pleased without needing to buy another ticket. It was a thrilling way to uncover the island's beauty and history. One stop that had a profound impact on me was Pearl Harbor National Memorial. I joined the line at the Navy stand, and, free of charge, we were ferried out to the solemn platform that hovered over the USS Arizona, still resting beneath the water. Standing there, listening to the haunting recording of that fateful day in 1941, I felt a deep sense of reverence and sorrow. History was no longer just something I read in books; it was tangible and real, echoing through the quiet lapping of the waves against the memorial.

Internet Photo

As my brother and I grew older, Mom started to let me babysit. I would often tune into The Twilight Zone, those eerie episodes etching themselves into my memory. One still haunts me: a story about passengers boarding a plane, some of whom had wings. It was a chilling realization of what their journey meant. To this day, I refuse to board a plane without my shirt that has rhinestones shaped like wings on the back, a small but comforting charm against the unknown.

One afternoon, Bub, my mom's partner, took my brother and me aside. He asked us how we would feel if he married Mom. Why not? I replied. She is happy, and so are we. He then asked if I would be willing to learn to play the wedding march on the harpsichord. I practiced day and night, my fingers stumbling over the keys at first but gradually gaining confidence. On the big day, I played that one song—the only song I knew— flawlessly. Mom looked radiant, and for the first time in a long while, everything felt perfect.

Introduction To Grief

But life, with its unpredictable twists, had other plans. Shortly after the holidays, Bub left for work as usual, kissing us all goodbye. None of us knew it would be the last time we saw him. He suffered a sudden coronary thrombosis and was gone just like that. The shock left us reeling. Mom, devastated by the loss, decided to move to a nearby town, Ansonia, Connecticut, hoping a fresh start might help us heal from yet another heartbreak. We found a small apartment in Ansonia, and I had to start at a new school. It was not easy adjusting to unfamiliar faces and places, but I tried my best to fit in. Mom, always resourceful, took a job at a photography studio. It was my first real introduction to the world of cameras, and I was instantly fascinated. The photography studio was in a bustling building, with a travel agency across the hall and a local radio station just down the corridor. The radio station, though small, often attracted big names, and it was not long before Mom's photography skills were put to the test.

One day, the station invited Hugh O'Brian to visit, and they asked Mom to take photos of the event. She kept us out of school for the day, and I could hardly believe my luck. I was about to meet a real-life movie star! Hugh O'Brian, with his chiseled features and charismatic smile, was even more handsome in person. He was best known for his role as Wyatt Earp in the ABC Western series The Life and Legend of Wyatt Earp, which aired for six seasons. He had also starred in numerous films, from Rocketship X-M to In Harm's Way. I shyly asked for a picture, and he graciously agreed, his arm around my shoulder as the camera clicked. That moment was pure magical – a cherished memory captured forever.

Photo by Mom & Internet

Not long after, another famous figure came to town—John F. Kennedy, Jr., on his campaign trail for the presidency. The streets were packed with people eager to catch a glimpse of the young senator. From our second-floor window, we watched as the crowd erupted in cheers, their excitement palpable. Mom, camera in hand, leaned out and shouted, *look up*. To our astonishment, he did, his gaze meeting the lens. She snapped the picture, a perfect shot that seemed to capture not just a man but a moment in history. Over the years, I would meet many famous people, but I always kept a respectable distance. Starstruck, yes, but their privacy was important to me, just as my own is.

As the dust of our new life settled, Mom found herself drawn back to what she loved most: singing and playing the upright bass fiddle. Grief is a complex emotional response to diverse types of losses and changes. In many cases, it is the feeling of being forced to let go or adjust to something that was once familiar or cherished. Grief is a powerful force; it takes immense strength to carry on, but pretending you are not grieving can be even more exhausting. Mom's smile seemed brighter now that she was playing music again, but I worried if she was truly coping or just putting on a brave face. Could she manage the emotional roller coaster of life while trying to be everything to everyone— emotionally, mentally, physically, and socially? She needed the band to heal, to find joy again.

Soon, she met a musician who played the guitar and accordion and could sing too. It did not take long for him to join Ruby's Ramblers, the band. I tried to be happy for her, but I could not help feeling wary. She had already endured so much heartache, and I was afraid of seeing her hurt again. I was only beginning to understand the permanence of death—Bub was never coming back, and his absence left a hole nothing could fill.

Mom took the initiative to start her own driving school, leveraging her multilingual skills in Italian, French, and Spanish. Her abilities quickly caught the attention of Avco Lycoming, who hired her to teach their foreign employees how to drive and pass the written driving test in the U.S. In addition to her work with the company, she also provided instruction at several local high schools. At the time, there was only one other driving school instructor in the area, a man named Jerry, which allowed both businesses to flourish. She thrived in her new venture, enjoying the opportunity to connect with a variety of people each day.

As time passed, the new band member became a fixture in our lives. He moved into our apartment, and for a while, things seemed okay. But slowly, his true nature revealed itself. What began as subtle manipulation turned into outright abuse. He not only manipulated Mom emotionally but also inflicted physical pain. It was unbearable to witness. My love and respect for her had grown tenfold through all we had endured together, but I was helpless in the face of his cruelty. After 30 long years, he never asked her to marry him, a fact for which I am deeply grateful. Mom deserved far better than the life she endured. Yet, for many women who experience abuse, breaking free from such a toxic cycle is a daunting and often overwhelming challenge.

To this day, I cannot bring myself to say his name. HE is just a dark presence that has overshadowed our lives for years. Watching my mother, who had already faced so much loss, enduring this new agony was heartbreaking. The strength she needed to reclaim her own happiness was immense, and though she stumbled, she never truly fell. She was fighting to hold on to the music, the one thing that had always brought her peace. For all the harm he caused my mom, fate had its way with him in the end. When he passed away, his girlfriend at the time took full advantage of him. My mom never knew about this, as she had passed away several years earlier. Karma has a way of balancing the scales.

My High School Years-Student Council

By this time, I was in high school, trying to make new friends and not be the new kid on the block. I decided to run for Student Council, giving me the opportunity to get to know my fellow students (also known as Networking) and tell them who I was. I was elected and served from 1963 to 1965. I took the secretarial course and that included home economics. I learned how to sew and design my own clothing, which included drawing my creations. Eventually, I designed and sewed my junior and senior prom dresses, and they were beautiful. In my later years, this talent would serve me well as an interior designer, not only in my personal life but also in commercial developments.

At that time, Connecticut was in the process of forming a professional football team called The Black Nights, and they were holding tryouts for cheerleaders. I had always been athletic, so I decided to try out despite feeling some nerves. To my delight, I was accepted. Becoming a cheerleader for The Black Nights was not just about performing; it was about learning the importance of teamwork, discipline, and persistence-skills that would shape many aspects of my life moving forward. Working alongside others, each with their own strengths, taught me how to synchronize efforts and support one another, both on the field and off. The Ansonia Black Knights were a minor league American football team based in Ansonia, Connecticut.

They began playing in the Atlantic Coast Football League in 1962 and played their home games at Nolan Field. The team finished fourth out of six teams during the ACFL's inaugural season and folded in 1964. Cheerleading taught me the importance of teamwork, a necessary trait for anyone.

I decided in my sophomore year of high school to try out for the Ansonia High School cheerleading squad, knowing that I already had experience with the Black Knights. All summer, I went to practice, and when school began again, I was selected as one of five Juniors on the squad. I was the only one who could do a jump side straddled split, and that was included in the tri-outs. Sixty-one years later, I would teach the words to that cheer to seniors at a senior living facility in Venice, Florida. Only this time, we all sat in chairs and did not jump or do side-straddled splits.

I had already been accepted into a sorority group called Phi Zeta Omicron. I was brought up as a Catholic, and once I understood what the sorority values were, I pledged.

PZO SORORITY

PHI - Symbolizes the grace of God, love as in philosopher or lover of wisdom, intuition, perception, renewal, and reform

ZETA - 8 key values are:

- Being Rather than Seeming.
- Humility.
- Leadership.
- Lifelong Learning.
- Love.
- Loyalty & Commitment.
- Responsibility.
- Seeking Understanding that We Might Gain True Wisdom.

OMEGA - Symbolizes the end of history and the ultimate destiny of humanity

Little did I know, I was the only member of the sorority who had the marks to even try out for cheerleading? I made the cut, and now I am an Ansonia High School Cheerleader. I was ecstatic and Mom knew how hard I practiced that summer. She went out and bought me a denim dress with red and white squares around the neck and sleeves. It was so hip and stylish. For the next two years, I had to keep my grades up to stay on the squad, and I had the marks to leave early for a part-time job. I needed a car, and my dad bought me a 1961 Chevy convertible red/white. (My introduction to my love of cars.)

I worked at Alexanders Department Store and started in the Men's Department and soon transferred to the Gift Department. It was then that I noticed the slanted windows above the department, and I asked what they were for. I was told that these windows allowed the security department to watch for shoplifters and that if I ever witnessed a shoplifter, I should not take my eyes off them, call security, and allow them to leave the store. Soon, a lady came into the store with about six children. She had a coat on that was extremely large for her frame. I continued to watch, and then I saw her take something and put it into the coat while the children tried to surround her. I called security immediately as I continued to watch her take other items. As she left the store, she was arrested. Her coat had pockets inside, which stored all the items she had taken. (My introduction to law enforcement.)

It was now my senior year. Mom got sick and went to the hospital for surgery. It was then that she asked if I could cook for my brother and the guy she was living with.

Mom never had me in the kitchen, so I did not know what to make. I found a can of Dinty Moore Beef Stew can said heat and serve, and I did. When I served it, my brother ate it, and this guy threw it at me and said some unpleasant words, and I knew then I needed to stay out of his sight. At the time, I was dating a senior who worked at a downtown men's clothing store. I would often go down and sit on the steps leading up to the store entrance to do my homework until I knew my mom was home. That winter was extremely cold and very snowy, and soon we broke up. I was a junior, and he was a senior, and to this day, I am not sure why we broke up.

I soon found out that the guy mom was living with found out that his girlfriend cheated on him with his best friend when HE was in the military. HE had major trust issues, and I was never allowed to be with mom alone. I knew that she needed someone, but I also knew that I would be graduating and would eventually leave home. It was after the breakup that I made up my mind to leave home once I graduated from high school in 1965. For the rest of my junior and senior years, I focused on my studies and continued to save my money.

Heading into my senior year of high school, I was not dating anyone, but that was perfectly fine with me. As graduation approached, I felt a growing sense of anticipation, like something big was waiting for me just around the corner. One day in early spring, on a whim, I decided to take my brother to the beach. I was driving my beloved 1961 Chevy convertible when he suggested I put the top down. We pulled over, and as I hit the switch, the roof folded back, revealing the bright blue sky above us. It was the perfect day. But when I tried to start the car again, I realized the battery was dead. As I pondered our predicament, I noticed a sleek 1961 Thunderbird speeding by. Moments later, the car turned around, and a tall, handsome man stepped out. He was like something out of a movie, towering over me at 6-foot-5 inches as he came to my rescue. His name was Larry, and after getting my car back on the road, he asked me out. I was thrilled when he agreed to be my date for the senior prom. Prom night, he turned heads as we walked into the dance, and all the senior girls swooned over him. They flirted shamelessly, and he, being the charming man he was, flirted back. Looking back, I should have seen the signs, but I was too young and naïve to notice.

Larry came from a wealthy family, and when I met his parents, they were gracious and welcoming. He was attending a military academy in Long Island, New

York, and every weekend, I would travel with his parents to visit him. We had so much fun together during those visits, sharing laughter and dreams of the future. It was a whirlwind romance, and I was swept up in the excitement of it all.

Graduation day arrived. Although I really wanted to go to college, I knew neither one of my parents could help me financially. A lot of my classmates were going off to college and some went into the workforce. I knew I just needed to leave home and start putting my life together, whatever that would be. On Graduation Day, and both parents sitting in the auditorium on different sides, I felt that the promise I made to both, graduating high school, was now fulfilled. Years later, I learned that many of my classmates never left the area, some still in their high school jobs.

CHAPTER 2

TRAVELING IN THE USA

With assistance from my brother, on the day after graduation, I left home for ventures unknown. My brother put a ladder up to the second-floor bedroom window, and I went out with a small suitcase and my mother's credit card. My new boyfriend picked me up in his car, and we were off! I left the car that my dad bought me for my brother. I knew I could count on my brother because he wanted the telephone that I had in my bedroom. This must have been a sign for him that he would eventually work for the telephone company and retire after years of dedicated service. Plus, he knew he had a car when he was able to get his license.

Our first destination was Niagara Falls, a place I had always dreamed of seeing. The sheer power of the water cascading over the rocks was mesmerizing, and I felt a thrill of freedom standing there, knowing this was only the beginning. Next, we headed to California, where my father's sister, Aunt Betty, lived. I knew she would help me get started.

California Dreaming

As we crossed the desert, we came across an abandoned dog on the side of the road. My heart broke for him, and I insisted we pick him up. We named him "Me Too," and he became our loyal companion for a time until I found him a loving home. When we finally arrived in Los Angeles, California, my aunt and uncle welcomed us, but their tiny trailer was far too cramped for us to stay. She graciously lent me some money to rent an apartment, and soon, we had a place of our own.

Larry found a job nearby, and I secured a position at a factory that made airport baggage carriers. It was not glamorous work. I spent my days on my knees, weaving strips out of fiberglass cloth and then handing them off to the seamstresses who would sew them. Later the strapping would be attached to the shell of the carriers to hold the luggage as they were transported to the airplane. It was exhausting, but the sense of independence I felt was worth every aching muscle. With our earnings, I paid back my aunt and uncle, and with what was left, I bought myself a car, a 1965 Mustang. It was not the powerful GT with the 335-horsepower engine I had dreamed of, but it was still mine, and it made me feel alive and free. Now, I did not have to take Larry to work every day.

Life in California was vibrant and exciting, filled with rooftop parties, beach gatherings, and strange new terms like *"bitchen."* The joy of driving that Mustang, even if it was not the model I had dreamed of, felt like a statement of independence and daring. My Mustang was definitely *"bitchen,"* a term that meant really cool in the local slang. I embraced the California lifestyle, living for the thrill of the open road and the salty air. One of my favorite songs at the time was *The Little Old Lady from Pasadena* by Jan and Dean. I had to laugh every time I drove down Pasadena Avenue in Los Angeles, knowing that the real-life inspiration for the song—a feisty old woman in her yellow 1932 Ford coupe— really did exist.

Of course, my love for speed got me into trouble more than once. I had a habit of flooring it at every green light; the roar of the Mustang's engine was exhilarating as it echoed through the streets. Inevitably, the red and blue lights would flash behind me, and I would pull over heart racing. "Do you know why I stopped you?" the officer would ask, and I would sheepishly nod, knowing I had earned another "exhibition ticket" for burning rubber. I collected quite a few of those during my time there.

But California. was not all sunshine, parties, and fast cars. The summer of 1965 brought the Watts riots, and fear gripped the city. I remember driving to work with my heart in my throat as people stood on the overpasses, firing guns at the traffic below. The chaos and violence were unlike anything I had ever experienced, and I was terrified every time I got behind the wheel. It was a stark reminder that even paradise could turn dark.

Watts Riot (August 1965) •

Internet Photo

After everything I had been through, I knew it was time to leave California. The allure of The Golden State had faded, replaced by a longing for safety and peace. It was time to start over again, somewhere new. Leaving California was bittersweet. It felt like closing the door on a chapter that held so much promise and energy. But I knew I could not continue living in fear, constantly looking over my shoulder. After Larry and I discussed leaving California, he informed me that he was enrolled at the University of Miami which was news to me. So, we packed up, sold my car, and headed to Florida; it made me realize that there were battles and dangers that I could not outrun and that sometimes, bravery meant knowing when to leave.

Florida – Sunshine and Flowers

Hurricane Betsy had just ravaged the state, making landfall near Grand Isle on September 9, 1965, as a powerful Category 4 storm, with winds exceeding 130 mph and a central pressure of 946 millibars. By the time we arrived, the storm had passed, leaving behind a surreal landscape. Our arrival in Florida was nothing short of eye-opening. The devastation was overwhelming, and Alligator Alley, the stretch of road connecting the state from coast to coast, was still under construction. We decided to head toward Ft. Lauderdale, following behind a bus, hoping it would lead us safely through the aftermath of the hurricane. As we made our way along the unfinished Alligator Alley, surrounded by two parallel dirt roads, we witnessed the raw aftermath of nature's fury—uprooted trees, scattered debris, and an eerie stillness that blanketed the land. Suddenly, the bus came to an abrupt stop, and the driver stepped out. We looked ahead and saw a tangled mess of downed trees blocking the road. There was no way through which we could drive. Just as we were contemplating our next move, a group of Seminole Indians approached us. With calm authority, they advised us to take the dirt roads running alongside the newly constructed highway. They even guided us to a crossover, ensuring we made it safely to Fort Lauderdale. It was a surreal journey, marked by the kindness of strangers and the resilience of those who had weathered the storm. Alligator Alley, with its dirt roads and unfinished construction, was a perfect metaphor for where I was at that moment: navigating a path that was still being built, unsure of where it would lead.

Internet Photo

Alligator Alley, officially named the Everglades Parkway during its five-year construction, had earned its nickname through local skepticism. Critics had mockingly suggested names like Swamp Pike and Alligator Lane, but Alligator Alley was the one that stuck, a testament to the road's challenging route through the Florida wetlands. It finally opened in February 1968, but at that moment, we were among the few to experience it in its raw, unfinished state, navigating dirt roads with the help of those who knew the land best. Once we arrived in Ft. Lauderdale, Larry, my boyfriend, left for college, leaving me to navigate Florida on my own.

Learning The Art of Simplicity

Determined to make the best of it, I found a job at a local department store as a floral designer. During the interview, I explained my current situation with Larry. Life took an unexpected turn when my supervisor asked for help with her son, who suffered from African sleeping sickness—a parasitic disease that causes swelling of the brain. We struck a deal: I would take care of her son during her work hours in exchange for room and board. It was challenging but also a blessing in disguise, as it gave me a place to stay and a sense of stability during a time when everything else felt uncertain.

My supervisor taught me how to craft arrangements that were not just beautiful but imbued with meaning and harmony. It was there that I was introduced to the delicate art of *Ikebana*, the Japanese art of floral arrangement. *Ikebana* was more than just a job skill—it was a revelation. For the first time, I began to see the world through a different lens. The Japanese philosophy of finding beauty in imperfection, of embracing the natural flow of life, resonated deeply with me. I had spent so much of my life trying to control everything, trying to hold things together, but *Ikebana* taught me that sometimes the most beautiful arrangements come from letting go, from allowing things to unfold naturally.

Ikebana is so much more than placing flowers in a vase. It is an art form that celebrates the fleeting beauty of nature, emphasizing lines, balance, and the space between elements. It taught me to see flowers not as individual blooms but as part of a greater whole, a living sculpture that captured the spirit of the natural world. This new skill stayed with me long after I left Florida, influencing my later work as an interior designer and shaping the way I viewed beauty and design.

One day, a Boy Scout leader came into the store with a palm frond and asked for a unique arrangement. Inspired by *Ikebana*, I used an electric wire cutter to shape the foam perfectly to fit into the palm frond, creating a striking composition that blended the structured elegance of the Japanese tradition with the wild, untamed beauty of Florida's natural elements. My supervisor was impressed and told me I had a real talent for floral design. It was a small but significant moment that filled me with pride and a sense of purpose. This was my first introduction to the way the Japanese purpose in life deals with the earth's beauty. Later in life, I would learn their purpose in life, or *Ikigai*.

Meanwhile, Larry was struggling at the University of Miami. He spent more time partying than attending classes, and it was not long before we decided to leave Florida and head back to Connecticut. The carefree days of adventure were over, and reality hit hard.

CHAPTER 3

FACING UNCERTAINTY BACK IN CONNECTICUT WITH NEW CHALLENGES

Soon after our return to Connecticut, I found out I was pregnant. The news should have been a cause for celebration, but it was overshadowed by the controlling presence of Larry's father and mother. We had a small, hastily arranged wedding, with only Larry's family in attendance. My Mom's live-in boyfriend (HE) forbade her from attending, threatening to throw her out of the house. I told her it was okay, not wanting to subject her to any more of his abuse. It was a painful decision, but I did what I thought was best to protect her.

Looking back, it was a time of contradictions—moments of beauty and discovery marred by underlying tension and uncertainty. I was young and trying to find my place in the world, but life, with all its unexpected twists and turns, had other plans for me.

During the day, Larry worked at a local fence company as an installer. I worked for Appliance Buyers Credit Corporation as a collector of past-due payments. I was asked to find a woman who owed a lot of money to local creditors, but no one was able to find her. I received her file and started the investigation. I learned she used to live in Maine. As I got further into the investigation and called different agencies such as trash pickup, tax collector, driver's license bureau, etc., I found her. During that week, the FBI showed up at work and wanted to talk to me. Seems that not only did she owe a lot of money to creditors, but she also embezzled a lot of money to open a senior living facility but never did. My first encounter with investigations, my second with law enforcement, and hearing about senior living facilities. I also worked at night at Howard Johnsons but soon I had to stop. I worked at the counter serving customers and the servers. One night, a group of four men walked in and sat at the counter. I started to take their orders when I realized I was waiting on Desi Arnez. I kept my cool, but I saved his silverware for a long time as this was not my first time around celebrities.

My husband, Larry, and I moved into an apartment in a nearby city; it was only about four months before my life took a dramatic turn. One day, I came home earlier than usual and found him in our bed with another woman. Overwhelmed by a mixture of anger and disbelief, I found a strength I never knew I had. I threw her clothes, which were scattered down the hallway, out the door and then confronted her. She soon found herself outside, joining her belongings. This moment was a painful wake-up call, one that forced me to reevaluate everything. I told my husband he had to make a choice: either find a real job or join the military, as he was a graduate of the military academy. He chose to enlist in the Marine Corps.

Amidst all this turmoil, I faced another devastating event. I began experiencing severe morning sickness, and soon after, I had a miscarriage—a little boy. I was alone in the apartment when it happened, and in my confusion and youth, I did not know what to do. It was not until I arrived at the hospital that I learned the full extent of my situation. The doctors informed me that I had been born with two sets of reproductive organs, perfectly aligned one behind the other. They also told me that because of this rare condition, I would never be able to have children. This revelation was heartbreaking, and I suppressed the loss of my child and the reality of not ever having children for fifty-nine years. I eventually channeled my pain and energy into building my career, focusing on the future, even as I carried this emotional burden.

CHAPTER 4

REFLECTIONS OF MY YOUTH

Looking back, I realize that each of these experiences, no matter how chaotic or painful at the time, was shaping me into the person I would become. I learned resilience in the face of adversity, the importance of finding beauty in unexpected places, and the strength to stand up for myself, even when it meant walking away from things and people I thought I needed. Life is rarely a straight path; it is more like that dirt road on Alligator Alley, full of detours and unexpected encounters. But it is those twists and turns that make the journey uniquely ours.

Knowing my husband was going away to Marine boot camp and what could have been a very lonely time for me living in a new state and not knowing anyone, I purchased my first White Shepard from California. Eventually, Walt Disney had a weekly program called White Shadow. I became hooked on watching the reruns of the series. White Shadow was an American drama television series that ran on the CBS network from November 27, 1978, to March 16, 1981. I fell in love with white shepherds because of their unique lack of traditional German shepherd coloring, their intelligence, their playful nature and their connection to humans. I named her Lady. Having had dogs all my life, I knew that I needed to train Lady. We worked for 15-minute intervals, and soon, she was obeying commands perfectly. Throughout the years, I trained several dogs. I found when training dogs, they respond first to taste or reward-based training methods, then to sound, and finally to visual cues. Hold a treat in your hand as you give the command, and they will naturally follow. As a treat, Lady received Cheerios. My deep love for animals and commitment to their well-being is central to everything I do.

After my husband completed basic training, we learned he would be stationed at a base in Charleston, South Carolina, aboard a submarine tender. To support us during this transition, his parents invested in a four-unit apartment building on Folly Beach, South Carolina. I managed three of the apartments while we lived in the fourth, finding a sense of stability in this new chapter.

While settling into the slower pace of life, I stumbled upon an unexpected opportunity: service members preparing to deploy overseas often sold their cars and motorcycles at great prices. I couldn't resist and soon acquired two remarkable treasures—a 1955 Thunderbird, a 1957 Thunderbird, and a 1965 Triumph motorcycle. The Thunderbirds were an absolute joy to drive, gliding effortlessly down the road. The Triumph, however, proved more challenging. Its heavily modified engine made it notoriously hard to start, requiring persistence and patience. Determined to master it, I began practicing on the beach, confident that the soft sand would cushion any falls. Those practice sessions were invaluable, teaching me balance, control, and a new kind of confidence. Eventually, when we returned to Connecticut, I purchased a stock Triumph that was much easier to handle, completing my journey from a novice to a capable motorcycle rider.

There were times when I wanted to go home to see my mom and my brother, but I remember how HE treated mom, and I could not live with that again. I really wanted to see my brother as well because we are close. Phone calls were great but different from being there with him. I finally convinced my mom to let Gary come down and be with me in South Carolina. I still had to go to work, but I thought the ocean was right there, and he could enjoy all that it offered. Little did I know he had different plans. He decided to raid my liquor cabinet. When I got home, he was on his way to being intoxicated. I decided to have a drink with him, but it only took him one more drink until he threw up. He learned his lesson and did not drink for an exceedingly long time. After my brother graduated from high school, he went to college and got a job with AT&T. At first, he tried out to be a lineman, but he was informed that he was color blind and that it would not be a good fit. So, he did office work. He started working in Mass. and soon was transferred to New Jersey and then to Atlanta, Georgia where he eventually retired after working at AT&T for 42 years!

CHAPTER 5

THE EARLY YEARS: FROM SECRETARY TO DRAFTSPERSON

After moving to South Carolina, I soon applied for a job at Avco Lycoming, and I was hired as a secretary working in the Configuration Management Department. The role of secretary provided me with foundational skills in organization, communication, and attention to detail. It was in this role that I first encountered the world of drafting. Intrigued by the technical drawings and designs that crossed my desk, I asked questions, stayed late to learn from colleagues, and studied every blueprint I could get my hands on. My curiosity and willingness to learn did not go unnoticed.

I soon realized that being a secretary was not to be my lifelong career. My boss saw this, and he asked what I saw as a career in my future. Directly across from where I sat was the Design and Drafting Department, a place I frequently visited for my current position and was intrigued by the drawings that they did. I thought to myself, could I possibly learn that trade? Unbeknownst to me, my boss, Norm, worked out an arrangement where I would be his secretary in the morning and work as a tracer in the afternoon with my mentor, also named Norm. First, I had to learn how to print, and I must have written the sentence: *"Lettering affects the appearance of the drawing more than any other factor"* more than a thousand times. The lettering had to be either vertical or no more than a 45-degree angle and a certain height, depending on what it represented; drawing lines had to be object lines, sectional lines, or dimensional lines, being able to depict a part in a layout and draw the three or more views of that one part, and learning how to read a scale (aka ruler). As time went on, I took night courses, studied independently, and continued learning on the job, eventually mastering the skills required to become a draftsperson. It was not a linear path, but I was committed to proving that passion and perseverance could be as powerful as formal education. Norm from the Design and Drafting Department and I became friends. He could tell I was overwhelmed by personal struggles and recognized my inner turmoil. Over time, he offered me a way out.

As I continued honing my drafting skills, life took another unexpected turn. I learned that my husband, who was stationed on a submarine tender in Charleston, South Carolina, would be heading overseas to Guam. During those long months of silence, the distance between us grew wider. When he finally returned, his affairs continued, and I realized I could no longer stay in a marriage filled with betrayal and heartache. It was time for me to move on.

I am living proof that formal education, while valuable, is not the only path to success. With passion, perseverance, and an unyielding commitment to self-improvement, it is possible to achieve your dreams and even surpass them. My career has been a journey of self-discovery, continuous learning, and the courage to take chances. If you can imagine it, you can do it. All it takes is action.

Life as a Road Jobber

As I was contemplating leaving South Carolina, Norm from the Design and Drafting Dept., a friend who had always been supportive, offered me a way out. As intriguing as it sounded, my only condition was that I could bring my dog along, and Norm agreed. I packed my bags, leaving behind my cherished 1955 and 1957 Thunderbirds and Triumph and headed to the airport. I checked in under an assumed name, something that was surprisingly easy to do at the time. No identification checks or security lines, just a boarding pass and a new beginning. I knew that his wealthy parents would try to find me using my married name. Lady, my loyal dog, and I ended up in Vermont, where Norm was working as a road jobber.

Norm's job meant he traveled from state to state, working on various contracts and receiving a per diem for his expenses. His current assignment had him living in a charming two-bedroom farmhouse with a small pond out back. It was a peaceful place, perfect for a fresh start. While he went off to work, I threw myself into practicing my drafting skills, determined to prove myself. Norm would critique my work each evening, and soon, he offered me a position as a tracer. I jumped at the chance. This was the beginning of my new career.

On the day I received my first paycheck, all six of us job shoppers headed to the bank to cash our checks, including the per diem we received for living expenses. In a playful gesture, we each asked for a silver dollar and tossed them up onto the roof of the bank as we left. It was a symbolic gesture, a little insurance policy we joked about, saying, If things ever get tough, we can always come back for the silver dollars!

As a road jobber, I quickly learned the benefits of this nomadic lifestyle. We were freelancers contracted through job shops like Kelly Services or Manpower but for detailers, designers, and engineers. The agencies did not care about your past, only your skills. Whether you were hiding from an ex-spouse, trying to escape a past mistake, or simply loved the thrill of exploring new places, this job was ideal. If you were ready to move at a moment's notice, you could experience the country one contract at a time.

I soon advanced from a tracer to a drafter, detailing each item in the designers' layouts. The satisfaction of seeing fewer and fewer red marks from the checker on my drawings was a sign that I was improving. With each assignment, my confidence grew.

When Norm's contract in Vermont ended, we packed up and headed to our next assignment in Virginia. There, we rented a small house on an island in Hungry Mother State Park. It was a charming little place with a tin roof, accessible only by walking across a small wooden bridge. I planted a garden to keep myself busy while Norm was at work, but soon, it was time for me to start working, utilizing my new skills in drafting. I will never forget my first day. I walked into the office, shown to my drafting board, and started working. Norm had been there for a while, and when the company's boss came out to greet me, he was visibly shocked. It turned out my job shop boss had only sent my initials and last name on my resume and assumed I was a man. I heard him in his office, furious, calling my job shop boss, demanding, *'Can that BROAD draw?"* Obviously, this was long before Gender Sensitivity Training was taught. He was given orders to fire me if I did not perform up to standard by the end of the day.

The next morning, I got a call from my job shop asking if I was still employed. Yes, I replied, holding my breath. Good, he said. Just checking. The contract I was working on involved designing modules for the military—seven units that could be airlifted and deployed in war zones or disaster areas. I was given the Dental Module to design, and I poured all my energy into proving myself. Each line I drew was a step toward establishing myself in a field dominated by men who often doubted my capabilities. It was a challenging time, but one that shaped me. I discovered a resilience I had not known I possessed and a passion for drafting that would carry me through many more adventures and challenges ahead.

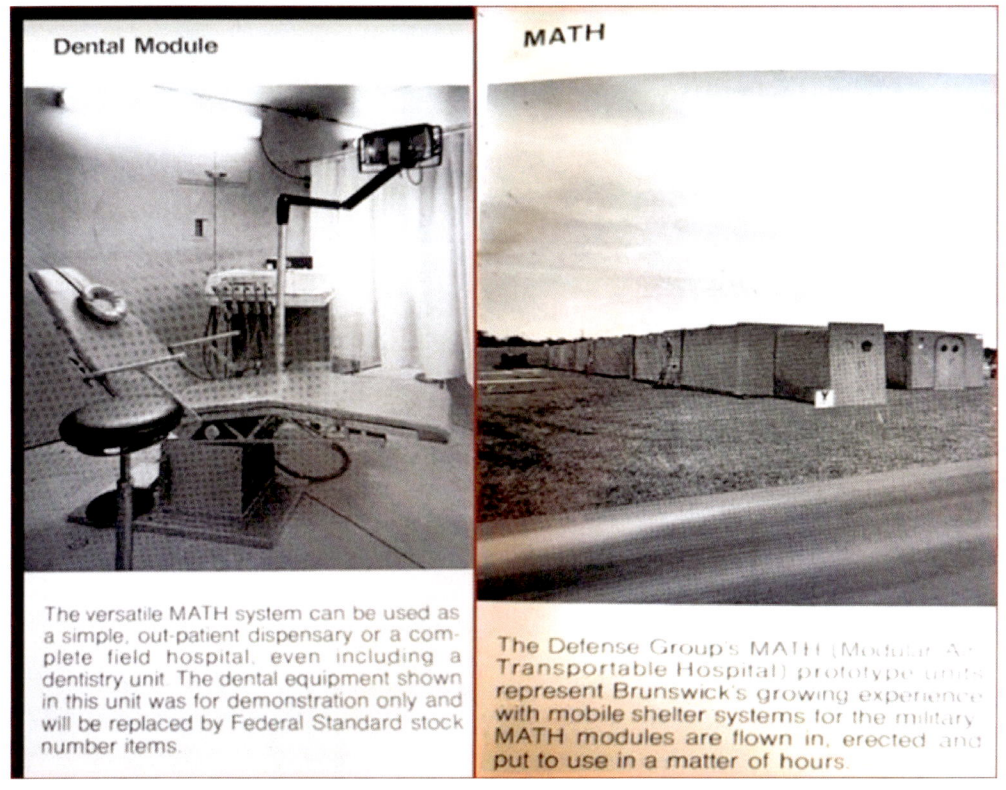

Dental Module

MATH

The versatile MATH system can be used as a simple, out-patient dispensary or a complete field hospital, even including a dentistry unit. The dental equipment shown in this unit was for demonstration only and will be replaced by Federal Standard stock number items.

The Defense Group's MATH (Modular Air Transportable Hospital) prototype units represent Brunswick's growing experience with mobile shelter systems for the military. MATH modules are flown in, erected and put to use in a matter of hours.

Images from BC Brunswick publication

After being air-dropped by helicopters approximately eighteen inches above ground into various areas, the unit was designed to expand into a full-working medical unit. When it came to one drawing called "The Polecat Assembly," I whimsically decided to draw a small skunk in the title block area. This eventually cost the company $500.00 when it came to bidding on the next build of the units. After the initial build of the first units, the military had to put the second bid out to several companies using the documentation we originally created, and whoever came in with the lowest bid would win the contract. Little did we know that one of the companies decided to deduct $500.00 for each mistake, such as an arrowhead left off, misspelling, or a picture of a skunk doodle they found off their original bid. The company that I was subcontracted with lost the bid.

Because this company had two divisions, commercial and military, I was offered a position on the commercial side of the building. This included designing my first low-cost billiard table and detailing some of the air hockey table parts. The Air Hockey Table debuted in Chicago in 1972, which was an instant success. Because I was a subcontractor, I had to sign an agreement that I would not be acknowledged in any design of a product. As I drew some of the items in the air hockey details, I was able to drill most of the 2,500 plus holes that were 1/16" in diameter and spaced 1" apart on the top of the Air Hockey table.

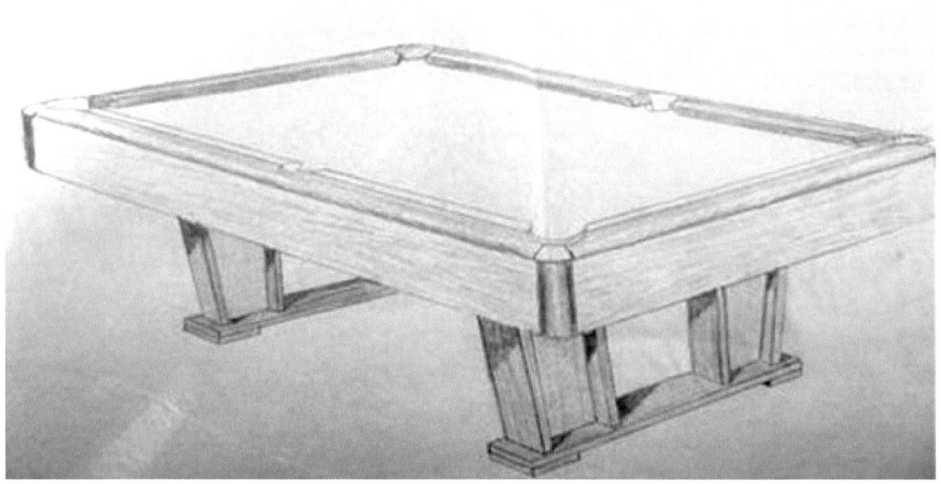

Photo by Linda Wilson

CHAPTER 6

BEYOND WORK: FINDING BALANCE & PASSION

We ended up staying in Marion, Virginia. For about 3 years (1971 to 1973). This town had approximately 4,500 people, a dry county, and about six millionaires. There were no nightclubs or theaters, but there was a beautiful golf course. So, being a member of the golf course, you were able to bring alcoholic beverages in and store them in the clubhouse and get to meet the locals. I decided that I needed an outdoor activity and decided to learn how to play golf.

I approached the golf pro, and he said I needed to go to another pro as he was fully booked. I soon found a pro that asked me, *"How serious are you in learning this game?* Growing up, I never had the opportunity to participate in many outdoor activities, so I reflected deeply on his question. I realized that I wanted to succeed in this new challenge, not just for recreation but to master something new. After all, many great deals and relationships are made on the golf course. I then said absolutely, I want to learn, and I am willing to put in time to become a good golfer.

From Hypnosis to the Golf Course

OK, he said. My first three weeks of learning the game of golf would be going to a doctor. *"Why a doctor?"* I asked. He will teach you the game of concentration. On my first visit, the doctor, who taught hypnosis, asked what I did for a living. I replied I was a mechanical drafter.

Hypnosis is a psychological phenomenon that can alter memory, offer pain relief, and modify behavior. Predisposition to hypnosis is an inherent trait, and some people are particularly responsive to suggestion. Using The Stanford Hypnotic Arm

Levitation Induction and Test, he explained the process of hypnosis and reviewed my treatment goals carefully. He would use a gentle, soothing tone, guiding me into a state of deep relaxation, describing calming images that created a sense of tranquility, security, and well-being. Golf, he said, is all about rhythm, balance, patience, and focus. But it is not just the game of golf; it is the game of life. You need to see it, feel it, and trust it.

"Are you open to this?" he asked, smiling kindly. "If so, I'd like to try a small exercise with you." Yes," I replied, intrigued.

As I relaxed into the session, he suggested techniques to help me achieve my goals, visualizing vivid and meaningful images of myself successfully carrying them out.

"Alright," he said, "I want you to sit quietly, close your eyes, and raise your arms out in front of you, parallel to the ground." "Let's get started," he said with a smile. "I'm going to teach you how to hypnotize yourself so you can focus on what you're doing and block out all distractions." It was transformative. He continued, "Now, imagine you're holding a feather in your left hand and a heavy dictionary in your right." I closed my eyes and did as he asked, visualizing the feather's lightness and the weight of the dictionary. After a few minutes, he told me to open my eyes. To my astonishment, my left hand, holding the imaginary feather, was raised above parallel, while my right hand, burdened with the imaginary dictionary, had dropped below parallel. It was a simple demonstration of the power of suggestion, and it worked.

As time went on, he taught me how to bring myself out of hypnosis on my own. Over time, I learned to practice self-hypnosis without assistance, using it as a tool to focus my mind and eliminate distractions.

After that, it was off to the driving range, learning the nuances of each club and the distances they could cover. Each week, I practiced with a different club until I had used all of them. As I perfected each club I realized they would all be in a small grouping when hit correctly. Most golf courses have a marker that is 150 yards out, often along with 100- and 200-yard markers to help you gauge the distance from where you land on the fairway to the center of the green. He taught me how to analyze a golf hole and strategically plan my shots using various clubs. Finally, after months of practice, he said, "You're ready for your first game."

A High-Stakes Introduction to Golf Game Called Nassau

Excited but nervous, I joined the local golf club. I did not know many people there, but the pro set me up with a foursome for my first game the following Saturday. They decided to play Nassau, a popular betting game on the golf course. A Nassau bet consists of three separate wagers: one for the front nine, one for the back nine, and one for the entire 18 holes. The stakes were high, but what I did not know was that the three gentlemen I was paired with were all millionaires. What I did not realize was that this was not just a casual bet. These gentlemen were major players in their fields: one had created a formula to preserve steel bridges, another owned several rock quarries, and the third had reinvented the soft drink Mountain Dew, launching it in 1961.

What seemed like a simple dollar bet was more like $100 or more! When they asked if I had any money, I said yes, though I only had $40 in my pocket. As we approached the 18th hole, we were tied, and my partner whispered, "You need to make a birdie." I froze under pressure and missed the putt. When it was time to settle up, I nervously asked if we could go double or nothing next weekend. To my relief, they agreed.

Victory and a New Path

I practiced all week relentlessly, using the hypnosis techniques I had learned to stay calm and focused. When Saturday came, my partner and I played a flawless game. We won, and I never played Nassau again.

I joined the Women's Golf League and teamed up with another beginner. We did exceptionally well, and by the end of my first year, I lost the Women's Club Championship by just half a point. My lessons with Pete had paid off, proving that with practice, patience, and focus, I could achieve anything.

Reflection

Looking back, the journey from the drafting table to the golf course taught me that success is more than just skill or luck. It is about the willingness to embrace new challenges, adapt, and keep pushing forward, even when the odds seem insurmountable. Whether in the workplace or on the golf course, I learned that seeing, feeling, and trusting in yourself are the keys to overcoming any obstacle.

CHAPTER 7

NEW STATE – NEW SKILL

Alta, Utah Adventure

Shortly after, my job ended in Virginia, Norm and I sent out eighty-five resumes, eighty to various companies and five to ski resorts. Norm, my mentor and close friend was a passionate skier who thought I would love the sport just as much as I loved golf. A call from Alta, Utah, changed everything. We packed up, including Lady, my 60-pound white shepherd, and headed west.

Arrival in Alta: Lady Meets Baron

As soon as we pulled up to the Peruvian Lodge, the owner greeted us warmly but with a hint of concern in his eyes. Lady is welcome here, but she will have to have a good relationship with my dog, Baron, he said, nodding toward the side of the lodge. I turned to see Baron—a massive, 200-pound Great Dane—emerging from around the corner. His size was intimidating, to say the least, towering over Lady, who was a solid but much smaller 60-pound White Shepherd.

There was a tense moment as they approached each other, both curious and cautious. As dogs do when they meet for the first time, they begin to sniff. Baron had to bend his enormous frame down to reach Lady's level, his long legs sprawling out awkwardly. The sight was almost comical - this giant of a dog splayed out on the floor, trying to be gentle and non-threatening.

Then, as if to break the tension, Lady gave a playful hop and a soft bark. Baron caught off guard, gave a startled whimper before his entire demeanor softened. What happened next was pure joy: Lady bounced around him, teasing and inviting him to play. Baron, clearly not used to being challenged like this, responded with a clumsy, playful pounce of his own, his massive paws flopping around as he tried to keep up with her quick, darting movements.

In no time, they were racing around the lodge, their playful barks echoing through the crisp mountain air. It was a heartwarming sight, this unlikely pair chasing each other through the snow, their joyful antics bringing smiles to everyone watching. No worries, I had melted away.

It was clear that Lady and Baron had formed an instant bond, and we had just received the warmest welcome Alta could offer.

Becoming the Alta Family

The following day, the dining room buzzed with the energy of anticipation as we gathered for our first official meeting. The staff, a diverse mix of ski instructors, ski patrol members, lodge staff, and even the owner, filled the room with excited chatter and an occasional burst of laughter. We were all strangers, yet there was an unspoken bond forming among us, the shared thrill of being part of something special in this snowy paradise. The owner, a man whose passion for Alta was evident in his every word, stood at the head of the room. He welcomed us with a wide smile, his voice carrying the warmth of someone speaking to old friends. Welcome to Alta, he began, glancing around at the sea of faces. You are not just employees here; you are part of the Alta Family.

One by one, we introduced ourselves, sharing a little bit about our backgrounds and what had brought us to this remote mountain lodge. There were seasoned ski instructors who had traveled the world chasing the perfect snow, wide-eyed newcomers like me eager to learn, and locals who had grown up with these mountains in their backyards. The ski patrol team stood out with their rugged demeanor and confident smiles, their presence reassuring and commanding respect.

The owner then outlined everyone's roles and responsibilities, emphasizing that while our jobs were different, we all had a common goal: to create a welcoming and unforgettable experience for our guests. When the snow starts falling, and the skiers arrive, they will be looking to us to guide them through their Alta adventure, he said. Whether you are serving them dinner, teaching them to ski, or making sure they are safe on the slopes, you are all ambassadors of Alta. He spoke of the unique history of the lodge and the community that had built it, reminding us that we were now a part of that legacy.

The lodge itself was a relic of history, originally constructed from World War II barracks. These had been hauled up the steep Little Cottonwood Canyon, reassembled, and repurposed into a cozy, welcoming haven for skiers. Alta's legendary powder, over 547 inches annually, was already piling up, promising a winter wonderland.

This place has seen countless winters, and each of you brings something special to it, he said. We work hard, but we also look out for each other. That is what makes us a family.

By the end of the meeting, there was a noticeable sense of unity in the room. We were no longer just a group of individuals from diverse levels of society; we were now the Alta Family, bound by the promise of shared experiences and the thrill of a season ahead. As we flew out of the dining room, the excitement was clearly visible. We knew that the coming months would be filled with hard work, laughter, and unforgettable memories.

That night, as we sat around the fireplace, swapping stories and dreaming of the adventures to come, it felt like we had known each other for years. The mountains outside were cloaked in darkness, but inside the lodge, there was a bright, warm glow of camaraderie. We were ready for whatever the season would bring—together. Alta was unlike any place I had ever seen. Learning of the torchlight parade, all staff members who were not participating stepped outside. The crunch of snow underfoot, the smell of pine in the air, and the sounds of encouragement echoing at the lodge. I was mesmerized by the torchlight parade on the slopes, a magical tradition where skiers descended the mountain in an "S" formation, their torches illuminating the snowy hills in a breathtaking spectacle. When all of the skiers finally reached the bottom of the slope, they all joined us poolside for food, conversation, and drinks. Skiing down that slope with the torches was the most beautiful sight I had ever seen.

One morning, after a massive storm had dropped 40 inches of fresh snow overnight, I let Lady out, and she joyfully leaped off the porch, disappearing into the soft white powder.

We all laughed as she playfully bound through the snow, loving every minute of it.

Settling In and Learning the Ropes

Norm quickly found his place behind the bar, charming guests and locals alike with his easygoing nature and infectious laugh. As for me, I became a chambermaid—a title with which I was not quite satisfied. So, I took it upon myself to rebrand as the lodge's very first "Linen Technician." It became a running joke among the staff, but I wore the title proudly. After all, it is all about perspective!

It was just before Thanksgiving in 1974, and the lodge was still closed to guests. We, the newly employed staff, spent our days raiding the kitchen, using the chef's pots and pans as sleds to slide down the mountain and getting to know one another. We explored the area, fascinated by the nearby Mormon genealogical records and the one bar carved into the rock—a place called "The Shallow Shaft."

From Snowplow to Moguls: Discovering a New Passion

The ski instructors took me under their wing, teaching me the fundamentals with a blend of encouragement and tough love. "Linda, plant your pole, up, down, and around", or "Belly button down the fall line!" or "Keep those skis parallel!" "Knees bent, and for heaven's sake, tuck that butt in!" they would shout as I hesitantly made my way down a gentle slope.

It felt like an impossible task at first, but I was determined. Day after day, I practiced, gradually moving from the beginner slopes to the more challenging runs. The thrill of mastering each new technique was invigorating.

Those days in Alta were some of the most exhilarating of my life, filled with new challenges, friendships, and the thrill of conquering the slopes. I discovered that, just like golf, skiing requires rhythm, balance, patience, and focus. And once again, I had found a passion that would stay with me forever.

Each morning, I would be awakened by the thunderous roar of Howitzer cannons echoing through the mountains, a signal that Alta Ski Area was actively mitigating avalanches. The blasts were a reminder of the delicate balance between enjoying the beauty of the snow-covered slopes and the inherent dangers they posed. Warm days and cold nights caused the snow to melt and refreeze, creating unstable layers that could trigger deadly avalanches if left unchecked. Several years earlier, the ski rangers had planted dynamite throughout the area, but not all the charges had detonated as planned. The entire ski area was closed that year until the snow melted and all the remaining sticks of dynamite were found. Only then did Alta reopen for the ski season, once again welcoming skiers to its legendary slopes.

Avalanche control at Alta is intricately connected to the legacy of World War II veteran Montgomery 'Monty' Atwater. In 1946, he introduced the revolutionary concept of using a Howitzer to remove snow from the mountain safely. By 1949, he had obtained approval from the U.S. Forest Service to evaluate a French 75mm Howitzer within the ski area's boundaries. This pioneering method laid the foundation for avalanche safety practices throughout the nation.

Internet Image

In 2023, a significant chapter ended as Alta's Howitzer retired after 75 years of service. This piece of artillery, which functions between a cannon and a mortar, played a crucial role in safeguarding countless skiers over the decades. Its retirement marked a bittersweet moment for the ski community, symbolizing the conclusion of a distinctive era in avalanche control. Today, they use a Remote Avalanche Control

System (RACS), which is said to be safer. The Wyssen system is a type of Remote Avalanche Control System (RACS) that utilizes a remotely deployed explosive charge that hangs above the slope to provide an air blast used to trigger avalanches in a controlled environment.

At this point in my life, I had found a fulfilling career and embraced two challenging outdoor sports—golf in the summer and skiing in the winter. I felt a sense of Icarian optimism, ready to take on whatever life had in store. But as the snow began to melt, signaling the end of the ski season, it was time to return to my drafting career. A call came in offering me a job at Bendix Corporation in Ohio, and soon, I was packing up and heading out for my next adventure.

Hello Ohio

Walking into Bendix felt like stepping back in time to the 1930s. My supervisor, who would later become a great mentor, greeted me wearing an apron, garters on his shirt sleeves, and a green visor perched on his head. The drafting room was bustling with activity—rows of people bent over their drafting boards, a sea of heads and elbows (to be honest, we always called them assholes and elbows) as they worked diligently on their designs. I took a deep breath and settled into my drafting table. The guys around me welcomed me warmly and asked if I played golf. I told them I was just a beginner and needed more practice before I felt comfortable playing with them. Practice, practice, practice, I reminded myself, echoing the mantra that had guided me through so many challenges.

I found a golf course about eight miles from work, Sugar Valley Golf Course, and decided to test my skills there after work each day. I felt a surge of energy and focus as I teed off, my training and self-hypnosis techniques coming into play. To my surprise and delight, after six holes, I was even par for the first time ever! Just as I was beginning to feel a sense of accomplishment, the golf pro came racing towards me in a golf cart. *"You need to get off the course now!"* he shouted urgently in his voice. Confused, I resisted, not wanting to abandon my game. But he quickly loaded my clubs into the cart and insisted I get in. As we sped towards the clubhouse, he explained that there were tornado warnings in the area and we needed to take shelter immediately. I had no idea that a powerful F5 tornado was about to devastate the town of Xenia, just eight miles away.

The tornado struck at around 4:40 p.m. on April 3, 1974, devastating the southwestern area of Xenia as well as the town center. It was one of the most catastrophic weather events in Ohio's history, leaving an indelible mark on the memories of those who experienced it or saw its aftermath. When I attempted to return to work the following day, the company closed, as everyone was involved in the extensive cleanup efforts. The destruction was staggering—80 percent of the homes were demolished, and 40 percent of businesses were wiped out. It would take nearly ten years for the town to recover and rebuild.

Internet Photo

As the chaos subsided, I realized my relationship with Norm was not moving forward. With a heavy heart, I decided to leave Ohio and return to Vermont with Lady, my loyal companion. I packed up my belongings into a trailer and drove back to the three-room apartment I had rented years earlier, finding it miraculously available once again. My trailer was filled with inflatable furniture—a living room set, a couch, two chairs, a bedroom set, a bed, and two side tables. It was not much, but it made the small apartment feel like home. I also had a small kitchen table and a single chair. It was a humble beginning, but it was mine.

I visited my former "road jobber" boss, who, knowing the challenges I had faced, offered me a job. He and Norm had been good friends, and he wanted to help me get back on my feet. I stayed for a while, grateful for the stability, but something inside me was restless. I was not genuinely happy, so I packed up once again and returned to Connecticut.

CHAPTER 8

HOMEWARD BOUND: RETURNING TO WHERE IT ALL BEGAN

Throughout the years, I stayed in touch with both Norms. Norm from Avco, sadly, died in a drowning accident along with his son—a devastating loss. Norm, the Job Shopper, remained a friend, and I was even invited to his wedding. He passed away in 2016, and I will forever be indebted to both for their support and friendship during some of the most challenging times of my life.

Life had taken me on a journey filled with unexpected twists and turns, from the slopes of Alta to the drafting tables of Bendix, from golf courses to tornado shelters, and finally back to where it all began. Along the way, I learned that resilience and adaptability were the keys to navigating life's unpredictable course. And no matter where I went, I carried the lessons and memories of those who had helped shape my path. While in Connecticut, I found a great one-room apartment owned by a local professor of linguistics. The house was a raised ranch with a separate entrance to the room, which became my living room, bedroom, and dining room table, along with a private bathroom. She and her daughter lived upstairs and thought that Lady would be a welcome addition to help with protection.

Cushman Contract Completion – Moving On

I applied and went to work as a drafter at Cushman Chuck Industries. I worked on the largest chuck that would hold pipes that were then drilled. The other designers and drafters loved to go out for lunch every day, and soon, they asked me to join them. The restaurant was a short walk down the street. At this time, there was no problem with getting an alcoholic drink at lunchtime. I had an all-white coat with fur around the collar, sleeves, and the hem of the coat. I also had knee-high white boots and a black shoulder bag to complete the outfit. Nancy Sinatra's song, "These Boots Are Made for Walking," hit the charts on January 22, 1966. Of course, everyone had a knee-high pair of boots; at that time, I felt pretty stylish.

The area of town was not the best, but I felt safe walking with the guys. As we approached the restaurant, I saw a gentleman come out of the restaurant with the same outfit. As we passed each other, he said, *"Hey, mama! Lovin the threads! Lookin fabulous!* Of course, I took a lot of razing from my coworkers, and from that day on, I never wore that outfit again. The guys and I formed a long-lasting friendship and met again in the next few years at other jobs. The contract soon ended, and I was soon looking for another assignment.

Colt Contract

I applied for a position at Colt Firearms and was hired. The crowning feature of Colt Armory is its large blue onion dome, topped by a golden colt statue that overlooks the district and the Connecticut River Valley. Colt Armory and its signature dome is a symbol of Hartford, the Colt firearm empire, and Samuel Colt himself, according to the Society of Architectural Historians.

At that time, I was working on the M-16 updates and process sheets. The name "AR15" today is used exclusively to refer to the semi-automatic (commercially available) civilian version(s) of the M16 and M4 assault rifles, going from the name of a single rifle to the generic name of a type of rifle that trace their ancestry to it. I was then transferred to the commercial division. Every lunch hour, I would either visit the historian, go to the underground shooting range, or meet up with some of the secretaries. I started tap and modern jazz dancing with a couple of women who also worked at Colt. We would all practice tap dancing and modern jazz when we could in the hallways. We ended up having our recital at the Hartford Stage Company the week after Bobby Darin's performance. Bobby Darin was an American musician, songwriter, and actor. He performed jazz, pop, rock and roll, folk, swing, and country music. Darin started his career as a songwriter for Connie Francis. Darin co-wrote and recorded his first million-selling single, "Splish Splash". By this time, I figured that it would be best to put my traveling days behind me and settle down.

CHAPTER 9

MORE THAN 'JUST A DOG': GRIEF, DISMISSAL, AND THE

DECISION TO WALK AWAY

The Loss of Lady

The bond with Lady was something beyond words. She was more than just a pet; she was a companion, a confidante, and, in many ways, a lifeline during a tumultuous time in my life. Lady came into my world when I was in the middle of balancing a demanding career and the personal challenges that came with it. She was my solace, a steady presence that made the quiet evenings at home feel less lonely. Lady was intuitive, almost as if she could sense my emotions. On days when work was overwhelming or when I was grappling with personal struggles, she would rest her head on my lap or nuzzle against me as if to say, "I'm here, and everything will be okay." There was a comforting routine to our lives together. Her wagging tail greeting me when I came home, our walks, and the way she would curl up beside me at the end of the day—it all added up to a sense of home and comfort that I desperately needed.

I came home one day to find her in distress. My heart dropped. There is a helplessness that comes with seeing a creature you love suffer, and you are powerless to stop it. The drive to the veterinary clinic felt like it lasted forever, my mind racing with prayers and desperate hopes. And when the vet took her in, and I was left outside, alone with my thoughts, I clung to the hope that she would pull through. But then, that strong breeze passed by me, and I knew. It was as if her spirit had brushed past me, saying a final goodbye. The reality of her passing hit me like a wave, and I felt a profound emptiness. The house, once filled with her presence, felt eerily quiet and devoid of life.

The Colt Revolt

Coping with her loss was one of the hardest things I have had to do. It felt like a part of me had been ripped away, and I was left with a gaping wound that I did not know how to heal. And to make things worse, my boss's comment, *"She is only a dog. Get over it,"* felt like a slap in the face. It was more than just a lack of empathy; it was a stark reminder of how isolated I felt in my grief. To others, she might have been just a dog, but to me, she was family. I quietly got up, retrieved all of my drafting tools, and left the building. In the days and weeks that followed, I struggled to find a sense of normalcy.

Coming home to an empty house was unbearable. I would often break down at unexpected moments—a song on the radio, seeing someone walking their dog, or just a quiet moment when her absence felt like a physical ache. What helped, though, was acknowledging that my grief was valid. I allowed myself to mourn, to cry when I needed to, and to remember her in ways that brought me comfort. I created a small memorial for her in the house with a photo and her favorite toy. It was my way of keeping her memory alive. The pain of losing Lady never truly went away, but it became a part of me, a reminder of the love and bond we shared. It taught me that grief is the price we pay for love, and though it is painful, it is a testament to the deep connections we make in life.

CHAPTER 10

PLANTING MY ROOTS – PROVING MY WORTH

Settling Down After Years of Travel

I left Colt Firearms and found a position at Scan-Optics. When I walked into their design and drafting room, I heard, Linda, where is your tutu? I turned red but the man yelling out was a former co-worker from Colt Firearms. His daughter, the other ladies from Colts, and I took lessons from the same instructor and performed at the Hartford Stage Company. I realized how important networking was, although, at that time, it was not called networking.

I started saving for a home. With the money I saved and help from my father, I found a place in Ashford, Connecticut. It was brand new and had about two acres. My front yard was the Yale Forrest, and there were only six houses on my road, and one of those residents was the mayor of Ashford. I moved in on Christmas Eve in 1976. It was cold and snowy, and soon, I ran out of heating oil. I called around and finally, a company came and filled up my oil tank.

The next day, I bundled up and went out to shovel my long and steep driveway. Suddenly, I heard a snowplow, and the driver stopped and said, *"Where did you come from? I* told him I just moved in, and he replied, *"Get out of the way."* He dropped his blade to the snowplow and plowed my long driveway. Lucky for me, the only reason he was there was because he had to get the mayor plowed out.

I realized how much I missed a dog, and soon, I was out looking for not one but two White Shepherds. I found them, and I named them Lady and Lance. Every dog I have ever had, I have called Lady or Lance. Not only did they become my family, but they would also keep themselves company. I finally had my *"kids"* to take care of. My house soon became my home. A house is just wood, concrete, and shingles, but a home is where you add your personal touches, turning it into a sanctuary. It was a charming Cape Cod-style house, with only the bottom floor finished: a cozy kitchen, a dining room, a bedroom, a living room, and a bathroom. With limited funds, I set about making it my own. I painted the walls and added rustic barnboard in the kitchen, giving it a warm, country feel. I had a Papa Bear wood stove in the basement and a smaller wood stove in the kitchen, perfect for those cold New England winters.

That summer, I participated in a city auction and won a bid for eight cords of seasoned firewood. I rented a log splitter and spent countless hours splitting and stacking the wood, feeling a sense of accomplishment with each neatly stacked pile. By Thanksgiving, I invited friends over and proudly prepared the entire meal on the basement woodburning stove. There was something magical about cooking with the crackling fire and the comforting warmth it provided, turning the house into a true home filled with laughter and the aroma of a home-cooked feast.

February 1978 brought The Blizzard of '78, also known as Winter Storm Larry. Governor Ella Grasso ordered the entire state to shut down as thirty inches of snow blanketed Connecticut, crippling highways and making roads impassable. We were released from work around 2:00 p.m. as the snow continued to fall, already ten inches deep. I cleared off my Datsun 280Z and began the treacherous drive home. The roads were eerily empty, but the front-end design of my 280Z plowed through the snow like a champion. What would normally be a 20 to 30-minute drive took me over two hours. Despite the power outages that lasted for days, I was warm and safe, thanks to the wood stoves and the stacks of wood I had split and stored. I was grateful that my grandmother had taught me how to cook on a wood-burning stove, a skill that served me well during that storm.

Before the blizzard hit, I had sensed a need for something to relieve stress. I stumbled upon a TV program featuring Bob Ross and his soothing painting techniques. I bought some paints, brushes, his art book, and small canvases. With nowhere to go during the storm, I decided to try my hand at painting. I was a complete novice and needed to learn everything—how to blend colors, manage brushes, and find inspiration. I found a picture of a beautiful rose in an old magazine and decided to copy it. I painted the background first, then the rose, its stem, and finally, the three leaves. It was a small accomplishment, but it sparked something in me. Painting became my escape, my way to unwind and express myself. Eventually, I even taught painting to residents at a senior living facility, sharing the joy and relaxation it brought me.

My 24-Year Career At Scan-Optics - Rising Through the Ranks

From 1977 to 2001, I worked at Scan-Optics in Manchester, Connecticut. Once I established myself as a competent draftsperson, I continued to take on more responsibilities. I sought out mentors, volunteered for complex projects, and constantly looked for ways to improve processes and designs. I initiated the Engineering Change Review (ECR) group, bringing together representatives from Sales, Manufacturing, Purchasing, Engineering, Design, Drafting, and other key departments to address concerns related to product design. The group met weekly to ensure cross-departmental input was gathered, fostering collaboration and improving overall design quality. Scan-Optics developed the image dissector tube and made it commercially available, pioneered an alphanumeric handwriting recognition system, and introduced key data entry integrated with optical character recognition via a direct computer-to-computer link to accomplish image reject repair.

In 1997, Scan-Optics' intelligent character recognition (ICR) developed significant improvement over standard ICR technology. Using 3,400 forms, Scan-Optics' ICR technology yielded a field read rate accuracy of approximately 90%, including acoustic double page detection, context editing, the integration of magnetic ink character recognition (MICR) and barcode reading into the recognition system and the introduction of grayscale capability in OCR. With that, Scan-Optics developed Series 9000 and Series 7000, which is a network-based scanning, character recognition and data entry system. Scan-Optics systems are used to process health care forms, federal and state tax forms, order forms, shareholder proxies, automobile registrations, credit card sales drafts and payroll timecards. The growth was also enhanced by Scan-Optics' expansion into foreign markets offering continuous support, training, and updates.

The Contract of a Lifetime: Where Passion Met Purpose

In September, the company received a $3 million order from a Health Organization located overseas for five image-scanning systems. It was time to align the sales promise with our technical capabilities while ensuring the solution was tailored to Japan's specific needs.

Over the next few weeks, I became friends with one of their engineers. His English was impeccable, and I admired the respect he showed to all his team members.

One day, I asked him why he chose to become an engineer. He explained that, from an early age, he was taught the Japanese philosophy of *Ikigai*, or "finding your purpose." As a child, he loved taking things apart and putting them back together, always wondering if he could improve the design and make it simpler or easier to assemble. He realized that this passion aligned perfectly with his career choice. *Ikigai*, he explained, is about balancing what you love, what you are good at, what the world needs, and what you can be paid. It is a philosophy that transcends not just our work but our relationships and passions, existing in perfect harmony. He also used the word *Kaizen,* which focuses on small improvements each day instead of trying to accomplish everything in one day.

Reflecting on his words, I saw the truth in them. *Ikigai* was not just a concept for him; it was a way of life. It reminded me to seek out and nurture my own passions continually, to find joy in my work, and to contribute meaningfully to the world around me. His story and the philosophy he shared became a guiding light in my own journey, inspiring me to pursue excellence and purpose in everything I did.

He then asked me, "What do you think your *Ikigai* is?" I did not know exactly what to say then, so I told him I would get back to him. There was a lot for me to process, but I wanted to give him the shortened version of what my *Ikigai* was. I took the weekend and laid out my *Ikigai.*

1. I love design. As observed by my manager at Avco Lycoming.
2. I am good at organization and management. I received the "1981 Outstanding Young Women of America Award", a program dedicated to recognizing and encouraging America's young women.
3. I wanted to be effective in the contract that the Company agreed within the signed contract.
4. The world needs this type of machine, but it needs to be easy to maintain in the field, low cost, and have more than one function to fulfil the required specifications noted in the signed contract.

Life is never complete and is constantly in flux. It requires compromise and honest conversations. Now I have my Ikigai, how would I implement my beliefs? I knew that this was not an overnight process (utilizing the methods of Kaizen), I knew it needed buy-in from all employees, and I knew it would be a challenge not only for each department separately but all departments working together.

My efforts of working harder than the person next to me and learning new skills with continuous evening courses paid off. I realized culture, collaboration and teamwork all make the company's culture shine. I was soon promoted to Manager of the Design and Drafting Department and Engineering Services. In this role, I was not just overseeing the work of others: I was actively involved in leading the team, solving problems, and driving innovation.

The Right People, The Right Results

It was a monumental achievement after winning the contract from the Health Organization, and we all knew we needed to expand our teams quickly. As part of the hiring process, I brought on three new employees, each one leaving a lasting impact on my life. The first was a talented designer who had just moved from Florida to Connecticut with his second wife and her two children. He possessed all the qualifications I required, and I knew he would be an asset to the team. The second hire was someone I had previously worked with at Cushman Chuck. I trusted his work ethic and dedication. The third was a young woman straight out of high school, struggling after the recent loss of her mother. She had no support system, so I offered to help. I picked her up for work every day and took her home afterward. After a few months, I encouraged her to get her driver's license and helped her buy a used car. Watching her gain independence was incredibly fulfilling.

The entire company moved to a new facility in Manchester, which accommodated all the new hires and included a showroom to display our equipment. A coworker and I were asked to decorate the showroom, a task I eagerly embraced. We reupholstered fifty chairs and soundproofed the room, creating a professional yet welcoming environment. This project sparked a new passion for decorating, particularly in commercial spaces. Our new location was ideal, right across the street from a gym. I made it a habit to go to the gym at 5:00 a.m. each day, then head straight to work. The area also housed other design companies, and it was nice to reconnect with colleagues from previous jobs.

Soon after, a contingent of Japanese workers arrived at our new building for an inspection. They filed in, with most senior members leading the way down to the lower in rank. After examining our first preproduction machine, they expressed concerns about the complexity of building, designing, and servicing this system in the field. I listened carefully and was inspired to find a solution. I wrote a detailed plan to address their requests. I thought extremely hard and thought of the acronym

Q.U.E.S.T. (Quality & Unity Empowering Scan-Optics Teams) to have continuity in our designs of the machines and to have less downtime when being repaired.

Now we had to get the buy-in from our employees. But how? I bought Frisbees with the initials Q.U.E.S.T., which stands for Quality, Unity, Empowering, Scan-Optics, Teams. Then we had a companywide meeting to introduce our new program. For the next two weeks, I welcomed employees at the time clock and if they could identify what the initial letters of Q.U.E.S.T. stood for, they received a frisbee. It worked, and soon, everyone wanted to be a part of the teams to develop a system at the grassroots level. Our Japanese customers were ecstatic with the new transformation of our new thought processes which would eventually lead us to having a quality product. The company realized that we needed a better software system and invested in a German-based software company called SAP. SAP helps companies and organizations of all sizes and industries run their businesses profitably, adapt continuously, and grow sustainably. The software collects and processes data on one platform, from raw material purchasing to production and customer satisfaction. After installation and training, it provided the necessary tools the company required.

Photo by Linda Wilson

Hard Work Equals Great Success

I created a plan and brought it to the CEO. He liked it and decided to form the Stability Committee, which brought together Sales, Design & Drafting, Manufacturing Engineering, Quality Assurance, Machine Shop, Engineering, and Purchasing Departments. We now had one of the major players together to identify what they did, what was needed from other departments, and what would help them go forward. This was an honest discussion about producing a quality product. By this time, the Stability Committee was reduced to five department managers: Sales, Engineering, Quality Assurance, Machine Shop, Design and Drafting and were relieved of their regular job duties. I recall that the meeting was held off-site and it was the same weekend that the Super Bowl was on. This was the start of the Triage Phase, stopping the bleeding and getting reliable solutions.

We needed to utilize the International Standards for Organization (ISO 9000). The ISO plays an important role in facilitating world trade by providing common standards among different countries. In the late 1970s and early 1980s, the developed countries of North America and Western Europe suffered economically in the face of stiff competition from our overseas customer's ability to produce high-quality goods at competitive cost. We also needed to implement Total Quality Management (TQM) regulations. TQM emphasizes that departments in addition to production (for example, sales and marketing, accounting and finance, engineering and design) are obligated to improve their operations; management emphasizes that executives are obligated to actively manage quality through funding, training, staffing, and goal setting. Once we had all the requests from various departments, we created a plan and presented it to upper management for their approval.

Once approved, we met on a weekly basis. This all started around the end of January. We also produced the idea that a training video would help our process. I took a course in videography, wrote the storyboard for the video, and enlisted assistance from another co-worker who would use the motion picture camera. That is where storyboarding can help. This video included Sales obtaining a signed contract and all departments coordinating their efforts from getting materials to inventory analysis to design and manufacturing, quality control, approval for shipping, installation, and customer training. This video was eventually used by our sales team for prospective customers. Doing this can help you create a more effective project plan and reduce the time it takes to get a team to sign off on a schedule. It is also a visual tool that many teams prefer to review, as a formal project plan is often hard to read and comprehend when it contains high levels of detail. Once all the information was gathered and we evaluated our findings, we found out it was working better than we ever expected.

Proof of Perseverance: My Educational and Professional Milestones

After four years with Scan-Optics, I received the 1981 Outstanding Young Women of America Award. This program, sponsored by leading women's organizations across the country, recognizes young women who dedicate their time and efforts to improving their communities, country, and profession. I was truly honored to be acknowledged in this way, knowing that these books, documenting our achievements, are preserved in state libraries nationwide. My only regret, I did not know who had nominated me, as I never had the opportunity to thank them.

1991 Introduction of the Video Writing Course.

Taking a course in 1992 with Progressive Management Association in Leader Effectiveness Training. I learned how to manage people, projects, and budgets, all while continuing to expand my technical knowledge. I earned the respect of my peers and superiors not because of a degree but because of my work ethic, dedication, and results. My philosophy was simple: work harder than the person beside you. That is how you can climb the ladder of success.

In 1994, I enrolled in a Plastics Design Form in which I received two Continuing Educational Units (CEUs). CEU is a way to measure hours of participation in an accredited program designed for professionals with certificates or licenses to practice various professions and immediately sign up for the Total Quality Management Training course offered by Davis Company.

In the State of Connecticut in 1998, there was the "Connecticut Award for Excellence – three levels: Nutmeg, Charter Oak, and Genius". I applied for the

Nutmeg level by listening to the needs of our users, providing quality support, and reducing system obsolescence through prudent research and development investments.

In June 1998, Scan-Optics, Inc. was notified the company won first place in the Connecticut Award for Excellence: Nutmeg Award for innovations to a product. It seemed as if I had found my Ikigai.

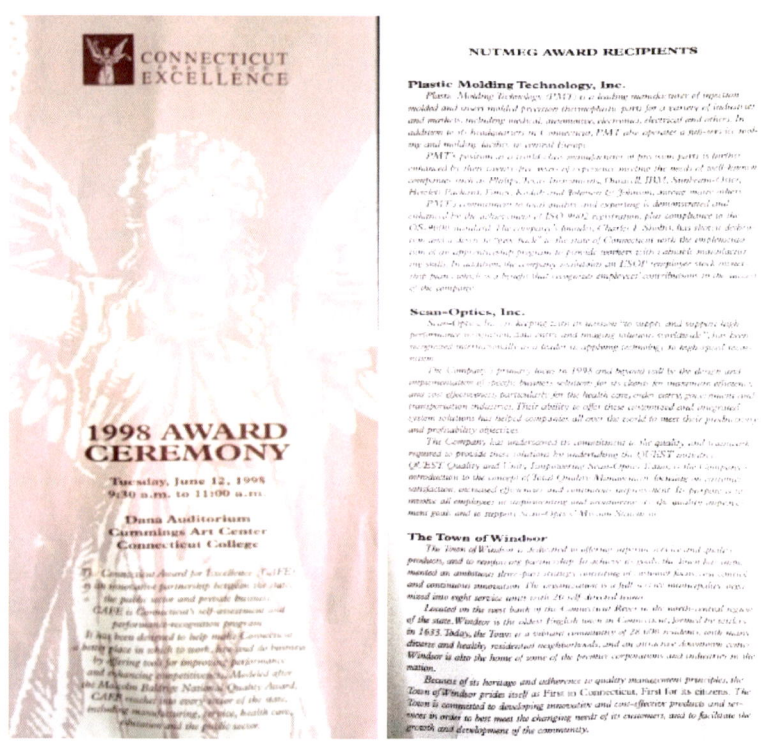

Photo by Linda Wilson

When Success Meets Sorrow: Navigating Career Triumphs Amid Personal Loss

My work life was going very well. But then, my personal life hit a roadblock when I was talking to my mother. I called my mom every Sunday and soon learned she had cancer. When she got cancer, I would leave work early and take her to her treatments. To make her feel better, I bought her five new dresses. She was delighted. HE never knew that I was there helping my mom, but it was only six weeks until she lost her battle with cancer. At this time, she was in Hospice, and I stayed with her. I remember hearing the Death Rattle. As someone approaches death, breathing patterns can change, and secretions may collect in the throat. This can create a rattling sound known as the death rattle. It is a part of the dying process and signals that death is near.

Soon, she was gone. As I was with her, HE came in and gave me a paper bag with the five dresses. I got up without saying anything and left and called my brother. Because she was never married to him, Gary and I had the responsibility of burying her. We decided to bury her behind her sister Mary's headstone, and we never told anyone where she was. It was time to move forward knowing now she was in God's hands. Her mental and physical abuse was over, and I was only hoping Karma would eventually catch up to HIM. It eventually did, but enough was said about HIM.

All three of my new hires were doing well. One day, the designer from Florida walked in, and he was in distress. He took me outside and told me that his wife was cheating on him. He caught them, and when she returned home, she pushed him down a flight of stairs. You could tell his ribs were hurting. He said he needed to find an apartment and needed to take the day off. Absolutely, I said. The following day, he was at work and living in a new apartment. As months went on, he seemed incredibly happy with his new life as he was now divorced.

The company was doing extremely well as the word spread rapidly though the OCR business community as to how accurate scans were, how downtime was at a minimum, and how easy it was to operate our machines. By this time, I ended up with 15 designers and two people in the Records Room working for me.

The Heartbreak of Layoffs: Navigating the Aftermath of Passionate Projects

As time went on, I could see the writing on the wall, and I knew layoffs were coming. All these people put their heart and soul into their work, but now all of that was going to change. I received a call from a vice-president to come to his office. Once there, he said, "I need you to lay off 10 of your people as of today", which was a Monday. He stated, *"You need to do this or get out of the way!"* It was the advancements during the 1990s that allowed companies to focus more on the software side of optical character recognition technology as opposed to making constant improvements to the hardware, which is what my department did. As I walked back to my office, I was debating how to do this, and finally, I called the ten people into my office and told them they were all laid off. It was one of the saddest days of my career at Scan Optics. At first, everyone was in shock, but then they said, "I know that this wasn't your decision, but let us take you out to lunch." I was so upset I just could not do it but I did say I would be in contact with all of them soon.

CHAPTER 11

SEASONS OF CHANGE: GROWING THROUGH THE UNEXPECTED

Times were changing, and soon, the drafting board was obsolete, and in came Computer-Aided Design (CAD) systems. My focus was selecting the appropriate system for both mechanical and electrical designs. In 1984, I attended Telesis Systems Corporation enrolling in their training program for designing printed circuit boards. It was then that I chose CADKEY for the mechanical computer-aided design systems. Originally released for Microsoft Windows in 1984, CADKEY was among the first CAD programs with 3D capabilities for personal computers. With SAP, CADKEY, and TELESIS systems in place the company was performing as a leader in OCR technologies.

Preventable: The Unnecessary Loss of a Valued Colleague

I was preparing for a long-awaited vacation, but first had to complete all the employee reviews. After submitting them, I left for two weeks, looking forward to a much-needed break. When I returned, I was stunned to find that my Florida designer, David, was gone.

I immediately asked what had happened. In his review, I requested that David receive a 15% salary increase, a combination of a new title with a 10% adjustment and a 5% company-approved raise, thanks to his numerous suggestions that had significantly improved the reliability and cost-efficiency of our products. His contributions were invaluable, yet he left without any notice. It was a shock to lose such talent, and I could not shake the feeling that there was more to the story.

Three years later, I received an unexpected call from an old co-worker. "Hi, how are you?" I asked, surprised to hear from him. He was doing well, but before I could ask anything else, he said, "I have someone who wants to talk to you. Confused, I waited, and then I heard a familiar voice on the other end. "Hi Linda, it's David, the Florida designer." "Wow, it's great to hear from you!" I replied, genuinely pleased.

David had since moved on to work at Hamilton Standard and was reaching out to ask if I could provide a sample of the paper we used at Scan-Optics. I agreed to give it to his neighbor, but he hesitated and said, "No, I'll meet you." We arranged to meet at a restaurant parking lot, where I handed him the sample. Afterward, he asked if I would like to go inside and have a drink. We ended up talking for hours. Of course, I needed to know exactly why he left Scan-Optics. Unbeknown to me, my manager at the time changed the percentage from a 15% increase to a 5% increase. Eventually, I showed him what I had originally submitted, and he was delighted.

As we continued our conversations, the music from the jukebox played softly in the background. Anne Murray's song "*Could I Have This Dance*" began to play, and he asked if I would like to dance. To this day, I do not know if he picked the song or if it was just a beautiful coincidence. Little did I know that this moment would change my life forever. When the evening ended, he asked if I would go on a date with him. I had always avoided dating anyone I worked with, but everything was different now. That night marked the beginning of a new chapter in my life, a chapter filled with love and companionship. David was a true Southern gentleman, and as we continued to date, he began to open up about his past.

CHAPTER 12

ROMANCE BORN FROM RESILIENCE

Foundations of Love: His Journey, Our Beginning

David's story was both heartbreaking and inspiring. He was born in Dallas, Texas, and moved to Florida with his mother and two sisters when he was eight. His mother, struggling with alcoholism, not knowing his mother changed their last name, and eventually abandoned all three children. They were taken to an orphanage by the Department of Children and Families (DCF), but when the orphanage discovered David had epilepsy, he was separated from his sisters and sent to a naval base to be used as a test subject for various injections, in hopes of finding a cure. It was a harrowing experience, and at fourteen, he ran away, leaving his sisters behind. As he made his way out of Fort Lauderdale, he met a young man his age who would become his best friend. This friend introduced David to his father, who took an interest in his situation. When David explained why he was alone, the man made an agreement with him: David could stay with them as long as he went to high school and graduated. David agreed and finally had a stable home.

During high school, David started dating, bought a truck, and worked tirelessly to restore it. But there was a problem—he did not have a birth certificate and, therefore, could not get a driver's license. His friend's father enlisted the help of a local investigative newspaper reporter. All they knew was that he was born in Dallas, Texas. After numerous calls, they found out that all birth records were in the Florence Nightingale section of Dallas Memorial Hospital, which had burned down, destroying all the records. They finally managed to get a copy of his birth certificate from the state, and that is when they discovered David's last name was not Mills but

Wilson. With his new identity and a valid license, David was able to secure a job through a work-study program at his high school. After graduation, he married his high school sweetheart, who was pregnant with their daughter. He found work as a drywall finisher, a skill taught to him by his best friend's father. He worked locally at first but then took a job that required him to leave the mainland. During his absence, his wife had an affair with his best friend, the very one who had helped him off the streets. When David returned and discovered the betrayal, he filed for divorce. On the day of the divorce, he went to see his daughter, who told him, "Mommy is with Uncle Danny in Texas." It was a painful realization, but he knew there was no going back.

David later married again to a woman with two children, and they moved to Connecticut, her home state. She worked nights as a waitress, and he took care of the children. One night, wanting to surprise her, he visited her at work, only to find her sitting at a table, locked in another man's arms, and kissing him. When he confronted her, she ran home, and David ended things then and there. His trust had been shattered twice, and it seemed like love was slipping further out of reach.

Our relationship grew stronger as we spent more time together. David began staying over at my house on Fridays. One day, he called me in a panic, saying there was an emergency at his apartment. I rushed over and was greeted by a terrible smell. All the windows were open, but the stench was overwhelming. It turned out he had tried to make boiled peanuts, his favorite snack, but had fallen asleep. The water boiled away, and the peanuts burned, filling his apartment with smoke and the foul odor of burnt oil. Everything was tainted - walls, furniture, clothes. We worked together to clean up, taking countless loads to the dumpster. Eventually, I suggested he give up his apartment and move in with me permanently. He called his landlord, who was happy to release him from the lease, praising him as the best tenant he had ever had. Little did the landlord know David had not been living there for weeks. From that day on, boiled peanuts were only made outside, and our life together settled into a beautiful rhythm.

On September 7, 1985, Hurricane Gloria made landfall as a Category 1 hurricane. Between the storm and other uncertainties, David began to question his future at Hamilton Standard. Our relationship was growing stronger, and we both knew it was time to take the next step.

The Proposal, Wedding, and Deep Diving into a Honeymoon

One morning, as we lay in bed, staring at opposite walls, David asked, "What are you doing the day after Thanksgiving?" Nothing that I know of, I replied, curious. "Would you marry me?" he asked, still looking away. I quickly rolled over and, looking at the back of his head, said, what did you just say? He repeated it, and I was in disbelief. This wonderful, smart, talented, and handsome man was asking me to marry him. It was not the most romantic proposal, but it was perfect in its own way. I finally found my voice, and with tears in my eyes, I said, *yes, yes, yes!*

That moment marked the beginning of our life together, a journey filled with love, laughter, and countless adventures. I had found my never-ending love, my true Southern gentleman, and I could not wait to start this new chapter with him. Planning the wedding was both exciting and overwhelming. I wanted everything to be perfect, so I asked David's daughter, Molly, to join me in picking out my wedding dress. It was important for her to feel included and to know that she was part of this new chapter in our lives. I wanted her to understand that we were becoming a "bonus" family and that she would have two moms who loved her dearly. The dress she chose was not what I would have picked for myself, but seeing her eyes light up made the decision easy. That dress became a symbol of the new family we were forming.

Next on the list was organizing the seating arrangements. We decided to make it more meaningful than just placing numbers on tables. The head table was named "Love," and every other table represented a key element of a strong marriage: Understanding, Compromise, Commitment, and so on. It was our way of reminding ourselves and our guests of what marriage truly meant to us.

On November 28, 1986, we were married in Ashford, with a close friend officiating after becoming Justice of the Peace. The ceremony took place at a local restaurant that had recently been remodeled, and I arranged for Connecticut's Governor's Foot Guard Horse and Carriage to bring our guests from the parking lot to the entrance. It was a snowy morning, and the soft flakes added a touch of magic to the day. Guests were staying at our home, and I eventually went to my maid-of-honor's house to get dressed. I felt a mixture of excitement and joy, knowing this was the happiest day of my life.

As my father escorted me into the dining room of the restaurant, where our families and friends were gathered, I was filled with a sense of gratitude and anticipation for the future we would build together. David and I had put a lot of thought into what we wanted our marriage to be. Just like building a home, marriage requires a solid foundation. We believe that the beauty of marriage lies in caring, with a love that grows stronger each year. The sweetness of marriage is in sharing laughter, hopes, and even tears. The strength of a marriage is trusting, with a faith that is constant and true. The comfort of marriage is creating a world that is uniquely yours, a home built on faith, starting with finding the right location that suits your architectural plans. Hope is to complete the rough framing, plumbing, electrical,

HVAC, and drywall. Courage is in finishing the interiors and exteriors. And love is the cornerstone, the final walkthrough of your home, where you receive a Certificate of Occupancy, or in this case, a marriage certificate that lasts a lifetime. And so, on that snowy day in November, surrounded by family and friends, we began our journey together. It was not just the start of our marriage; it was the beginning of a life filled with love, laughter, and the promise of forever.

Later, I asked David why he chose the day after Thanksgiving for our wedding. He smiled and said, *"Because I'll always remember our anniversary."* It was a thoughtful gesture, but he had not realized that the date would change every year. So, we made it a tradition to celebrate our anniversary the day after Thanksgiving, regardless of the actual date. We decided to delay our honeymoon because we had guests visiting from Vermont and Georgia. Instead, we took a trip to Sandals Resort in Jamaica several months later. The resort was breathtaking, with a waterfall cascading down a brick wall near the entrance and multiple pools, including a swim-up bar. There were endless activities, and we decided to qualify for diving. Our instructor, an ex-Navy SEAL named Stereo, guided us through the process. We first practiced in the pool, where they calculated the weight needed for us to dive. Then, we headed to the beach for a swim test. David, a natural swimmer and former surfer, completed the test effortlessly. I, on the other hand, struggled.

Stereo swam up to me and encouraged me, you can do this. I somehow managed to complete the swim, and we prepared for our first dive. The next day, we dove to about twenty feet, feeding the vibrant fish and exploring the coral reefs. Stereo humorously used hand signals to describe the marine life we might encounter. He formed a circle with his hands on his head to represent an angel fish and made other gestures for different species. Then, he put his thumb toward his palm and made a fin on his head, indicating a shark. "If you see this," he said, "I'm out of here, and you're on your own." We all laughed, but there was a hint of seriousness in his tone. When it was time to dive, we sat on the edge of the boat, fully geared, and fell backward into the water. Holding onto the rope that anchored the boat, we began our descent. As each diver let go of the rope, they swam gracefully downward—all except me. For some reason, my body decided to float butt-first to the surface. After a quick adjustment with some extra weight, I was finally able to join the group, swimming among the fish and marveling at the underwater world.

From Honeymoon to New Endeavors

When we returned from our honeymoon, it was back to reality. I noticed the long drive from Ashford to Hamilton Standard was taking a toll on David and his Thunderbird. The final straw came when his car broke down on the interstate. It was time for a new vehicle. David meticulously crafted a list of specifications for his dream truck. When he presented it to the dealer, they were initially skeptical that such a truck could be ordered. But six weeks later, we had a 1998 Dodge Ram 2500 diesel with a towing package. It was black and red, and we proudly named it "Big Red." Little did I know this truck was part of David's plan to return to construction, a field he had always loved. We decided to start our own business, D&L Drywall. David handled the estimating, hanging, and finishing of the drywall, while I managed the ordering and scheduling while I remained at Scan-Optics. Our first job was for our best man and maid-of-honor, who owned a residential building company. They were constructing a new home for themselves, a 5,000-square-foot masterpiece with lofty ceilings and an octagon-shaped breakfast area. We ordered all the drywall and a scissor lift, and confidently, we would be hired for the job. But after submitting our bid, they chose a cheaper company. It was a blow, but we returned the lift and moved on. A month later, the new drywall company contacted David, asking him to finish the job they had started. It was an insult he could not overlook. He declined and wished them luck.

Meanwhile, I was also reconnecting with my love of golf. One day, a coworker asked if I could fill in for his partner at the Scan-Optics Golf League. Although I had not played in a while and did not have my clubs, he insisted. My boss gave me permission to leave work early, so I retrieved my clubs and headed to the course. Before teeing off, I asked if they preferred I play from the women's or men's tee box. They chose the women. The silence was deafening as I lined up my shot. I turned and said, "You can make some noise if you want." With a calm swing, I hit the ball perfectly down the fairway. After three pars in a row, my partner asked if I would join him permanently. His current partner was being transferred, and he needed someone reliable. For the next five years, we dominated the league, taking first place each season.

By this time, David had decided to work for someone else, taking a year-round job that kept him busy even during the harsh Connecticut winters. He loved to joke around with his coworkers. On snowy days, he stood inside and pretended to wipe sweat from his brow, teasing the other tradesmen working outside. His sense of humor was one of the many things I adored about him.

When I first met David, his hair was a rich brown with just a hint of gray. But over time, the gray took over. One day, he came home and asked if I could try a temporary hair color on him, thinking it might make him look younger. I did not realize I had that kind of effect on people. That summer, he was working on a church steeple in the dead heat of July. When he arrived at the site with his newly colored hair, no one recognized him at first. He hopped on the scissor lift and headed up to the steeple. But by the time he came down, the intense heat had caused the color to drip down his face. He looked like a cross between a clown and Alice Cooper. We laughed about it for weeks, and he never asked me to color his hair again!

CHAPTER 13

PIECES OF THE PAST:

A QUEST TO FIND DAVIDS' PARENTS

Finding His Mom

As winters in Connecticut became increasingly harsh, with bitter cold and heavy snow, David started thinking about his past and his family. He told me he wanted to find his birth parents and gain some closure. My investigative skills kicked into high gear, and we started piecing together everything he could remember. For the next ten years, we dedicated ourselves to finding his birth parents. Every week, David would come to Scan-Optics, and we would spend hours on the Wide Area Telephone Service (WATS) line, calling people all over the country. Finally, we found his mother living in a low-income apartment in Oklahoma City. She was different from how David remembered— no longer drinking but relying on food stamps and living in poverty. We sent her some money, which she kept in aluminum foil in her freezer, calling it her "Alcoa Funds." She told us that David's father had died in a car accident, but something about her story did not add up.

David's daughter was now married with a son, and we decided to fly everyone to Oklahoma City to meet his mother. I captured a rare and cherished photograph of five generations: David's grandmother, his mother, David, his daughter, and her son. It was a bittersweet moment, as his mother was on oxygen and still smoking despite our concerns. On Christmas morning, we received a devastating call. She had lit a cigarette, and the oxygen tank exploded. She was gone. Before her death, we had managed to locate David's two sisters.

We bought airline tickets for them to attend the funeral, and it was the first time David had seen them since they were separated at the orphanage. They both wanted to know why he had not taken them with him when he ran away. David explained that he could barely take care of himself at the time. After a difficult conversation, they forgave him.

Sadly, we later learned that his older sister had committed suicide. She had distanced herself from the family, and we discovered she had a different father. His younger sister had moved to Colorado, where she met a trucker. She decided to leave her son in Florida and moved to Alaska with him to start a new life. Despite the distance, she and David stayed in touch, and eventually, we traveled to Alaska to meet her and her new family. Alaska was stunning, especially in July, during salmon season. Every morning, we would check reports on the salmon swimming up the Kenai River to spawn. David's sister was a true outdoorswoman, and she and David would go fishing together. We even bought her a smoker so she could perfect her special recipe for smoked salmon. It was delicious. She shared stories of moose hunting and how she used to bring the moose into her tiny log cabin to butcher it on the kitchen table. Once they saved enough money to expand their home, the kitchen was no longer the butchering area!

Finding His Dad

Next, it was time to find David's father. For ten years, we searched everywhere we thought he might be. His name seemed unique, or so we thought, and we contacted everyone we could think of—libraries, trash collectors, tax collectors, you name it. After watching a talk show, we learned about U.S. Search, a CA-based agency that helps people find lost relatives. We contacted them, and they sent us a list of 60 people with his father's name. Only one did not have an address or phone number. We called the other 59 names to no avail. The chances seemed slim, but we had to try the last one. It was Good Friday, May of 1996, when I called the Assessor's Office in Joplin, Missouri. I was not sure they would be open, but the call was answered. I explained why I was searching and asked if they knew the name. The woman on the line could not confirm it but suggested I call a woman with the same last name. I thanked her and found the phone number online. I was excited and nervous as I dialed, hoping for a breakthrough. David and I were in separate rooms, frustrated from years of searching. I handed him the phone and said, *"Here, this might be your dad. "* When the person on the other end answered, there were noises in the background, like the sound of an old gas station bell when a car ran over a wire. The man asked if he could hold for a moment while he went inside. When he returned, he asked, "What did you say?" David said, *"I think that you might be my father. Were you married to Billie Jean, and is your name such and such?"* Yes, the man replied. Then he added, *"Oh my God, son, where have you been? "* It had been 42 years since they had last seen or spoken to each other.

They spent hours talking on the phone that day, and soon, David received calls from cousins he never knew he had. We planned a trip to Joplin to meet his father. The day finally came, and as we pulled into his driveway, we saw his dad running down the long, steep incline. David stopped the car, and his dad yanked open the door and pulled him out, hugging him tightly. They were both incredibly strong men, and it was like watching a reunion that time itself had tried to prevent.

I could not help but notice the similarities. They were both wearing similar shirts, drove the same type of van, and even owned the same model, Mercedes. Both had impeccably clean, very white sneakers. It was uncanny. A local newspaper reporter showed up that afternoon and wanted to do a feature article on their reunion. The story appeared in the *Our Neighborhood* section of the paper with the headline: *Together Again!* It was a moment of pure joy and healing. What made me smile was the front page of *"The Joplin Globe."* Like many newspapers, there is a section where the headline stories summarizes various articles throughout the paper. If one read it quickly, all one saw was: "Gay Marriages", and just below was David and his dad's picture with the headline: "Dad, son reunited." It was as if the universe had finally conspired to bring them together, and the whole world was bearing witness to their long-awaited reunion with a little humor added in if you only read the headlines and looked at the picture.

Photos from Joplin Newspaper

His dad went to the butcher shop to order steaks, and all his cousins came to visit, as well as meeting his stepsister and stepbrother. The meeting with his stepsister and stepbrother did not go well. They pulled David aside and asked what David's real intentions were. David said, *"I am his firstborn, and I deserve to know my dad."* Little did we know that his wife had Power of Attorney and changed his dad's will, not that it meant anything to David, and he and his sisters were specifically written out of his dad's will. The visit was everything David was hoping for except for his stepsibling and his wife.

David, his dad, and I went up to Alaska to have him meet his youngest daughter. She was not as accepting of his affections because she thought her dad should have made more of an effort to find the three kids. For the next couple of years, David and his dad talked frequently. We soon learned that his oldest sister was a half-sister. We tried to locate her but could not. She had her issues, and we soon learned that she died on Christmas Day.

On May 11, 1998, his dad passed away. We immediately flew to Joplin, Missouri. In the church, his brother said, *"Don't think that you're getting anything from my dad."* We turned around and found a seat in church. His cousins all had beautiful voices, and each one gave their eulogy as to what their uncle meant to them at the church podium. They also included how happy their uncle was after reuniting with David. His dad was buried, David and I left, and he never spoke to his stepbrother again. David finally had closure. Life in Connecticut was good, but David was having difficulty dealing with the snow and ice. We discussed moving to Florida but on the West Coast.

CHAPTER 14

GOODBYE SNOW – HELLO SUNSHINE

We finally sold our home, moved to Sarasota, Florida, and rented an apartment. We arrived in Florida on Sept. 10, 2001, the day before the 9/11 attacks. It had to be fate that we left when we did, having major help from our friend, Glenn. Glenn helped us pack up our belongings and took time off from work. In exchange for his help, we bought him an airline ticket to return to Connecticut. Glenn had a fear of flying, but there was not anything he would do for David or me. Glenn was like the brother David never had. Despite their differences, they always had each other's backs. Glenn worked at a timber company operating heavy machinery and was usually seen in jeans and a black cut-off T-shirt. Raised on a farm with livestock, he was the rugged type—a hunter who put food on the table, butchered livestock, harvested hay, and grew vegetables in the family garden. No one dared to mess with him. To this day, Glenn has always been there for me, and I will always appreciate and love him!

Photo by Linda Wilson

David, on the other hand, had a knack for design and technology. He specialized in designing printed circuit boards and worked as a skilled drywall tradesman. Through dedication and hard work, he rose through the ranks at Hamilton Standards, eventually managing a team of ten designers. Finally, after the 9/11 attacks, the airlines were back in operation, and Glenn was able to fly back home. As time went on, Glenn visited us in Venice, but his fear of flying had never left him. My dad moved to Florida with us. David needed some time off, so the three of us went fishing together. This was David's love of outdoor sports.

Seeking Employment & Home

David soon realized he needed to get a paying job, and I would start looking for a home to buy. David applied to a drywall company and had an interview with the owner. When David talked to him and told him what hourly wage he was getting in Connecticut, and expected the same in Florida. The owner of the drywall company fell back in his chair and grabbed his heart. David said to the owner, *"Thank you for your time",* and got up to leave. As he approached the door, the owner said, *"I will tell you what. Come in tomorrow and meet with my top guy."* David complied, and when he showed up the following day, he asked what the top guy wanted him to do. It was an apartment building, and David could take one side of the complex, and he would take the other side on the same floor. As David finished his assigned side of the apartment complex, he sought out his boss. When he finally found him, he was shocked to see David, and more so that he completed his side of the apartment floor. This guy wanted to see if he was done with the first coat, as he had only completed half of his side of the floor.

When he walked into the first apartment, he asked David what those tools were laying on the floor. David said they are called "Ames Tools" which is a tool that holds joint compound, drywall tape, and fitted with a cutting tool and folding tool for the drywall tape. It was about three feet long and weighed about 50 pounds when full of joint compound and held 5,000 feet of drywall tape. His boss had never seen one, let alone know how to operate it. David went into an unfinished room and showed his boss how to use it. Flabbergasted, his boss went back to the owner of the company and said, you better hire this guy. I called him "Super Dave", and that name stuck from that point on. David went on to teach all the other finishers how to use the tools, increased production time and soon received the same amount of pay he received in Connecticut. Super Dave became a supervisor for the company about two weeks after he joined.

Being creative on a Budget

It was time for us to find a home. As David left work, I realized he had forgotten his lunch. I said to my dad, let us take a ride to Venice and bring David his lunch. On our way back to Sarasota, I noticed a new development being constructed and asked my dad if he wanted to stop in. We did. We looked at various models. There were three builders in the development, and each had its unique style. The realtor took us through the Phase II building area, and I saw a property that was meeting all the criteria David, and I discussed. I told her I wanted to put a deposit down, and I did. Before David left work that day, I said I wanted to meet him. He was the new owner of a piece of property! At first, he was not happy because we always discussed things before we made any decisions. But when he saw the property, his attitude changed. Later, we learned three other people had expressed interest in the property that afternoon. We closed on the land in December. We decided to have our bank dole out the money in the three phases of construction and not have the builder use our money. New laws came into effect regarding home construction in Florida, including the requirement for hurricane tie-down brackets to secure roof trusses to the main structure. I thoroughly researched Florida's new Code Enforcement Rules. Hurricane ties are metal connectors used to secure roof trusses or rafters to the building's supporting walls or other structural elements, providing essential lateral support to prevent the roof from detaching in high winds. They also help resist uplift forces on the roof. Additionally, all vegetation must now be planted at least 18 inches from the home's walls, allowing rainwater to reach the plants directly. Previously, plants were placed close to the walls, where gutters would direct rainwater to city sewers; this setup also attracted bugs that could eventually enter the home.

As construction on our home began, I was on-site every day, staying informed about progress and keeping the supervisor aware of any issues or questions I had after reviewing the blueprints. For example, one closet was not framed correctly, the plywood sheathing was not fully nailed down to the trusses after the roofers left, and some overhead water pipes in the master bathroom had not been connected. I stayed out of the way of subcontractors and maintained a detailed list of items needing attention. At the time, the builder seemed appreciative. Construction demand was just beginning to surge, and we managed to start our building before housing prices began to climb. At the end of the building cycle, as we went to our closing, the builder stated that it was the first time in his career that he owed money to the client. My record-keeping was solid, and I kept the builder informed. We moved into our new home in September of 2002. Just before that winter, I invited my aunt to also live with us. She had lost her husband and was going to move into an apartment. When she was given the key to the apartment, she could not open the door. I believe, as she did that this was a sign for her to come and live with us.

Now, it was time to make this our home. Paint the walls first and then start to add the charm I thought both of us liked. Our ceilings in the bedroom and the family room were stepped but were not that noticeable due to the same paint colors as the walls. I grabbed my paint and brushes and went to work on the ceiling. Taking cream, white, and light brown, I modeled the paint. It was now definitely noticeable. In the family room there are two shades of green in the double step of the ceiling.

I first went to a big box store and to the woodworking area. We already had an entertainment center, and I noticed on the edges that it looked like dowels glued together with a caning wrapped in an "X." I saw long pieces of ¼ inch molding you would put on the floor that meets the wall. I went to the scrap area, took two pieces, and held them together, forming a ½ inch round. Then I took several pieces of dowels and placed them on the two pieces of ½ inch molding. It looked just like my entertainment trim. Now for the "X" on the assembly. I had caning from a previous project, and once I wet the caning, I was able to form it to create the look I wanted. Once assembled, I stained all the pieces. It was perfect! It was time to install it on the step-down ceiling. What a difference!

FIGURE 1

2 ¼" ROUNDS GLUED W/DOWELS

FIGURE 2

CORNER OF ENTERTAINMENT CENTER

FIGURE 3

LOCATED ON STEPPED CEILING

Photos by Linda Wilson

We had a triple sliding glass door in the living room. I started to check the prices of curtain rods. Totally out of the question. Went back to the big box store in the closet pole section. I bought one 14-foot pole and some wood putty. I took rubber bands and placed them approximately 14 inches apart. I have always loved the look of bamboo and decided that is what I was going to make. I took the wood putty and started to form the "knuckles" on each side of the rubber band. Once all the knuckles were formed, I began the fun part of creating the look of bamboo. I painted the entire closet pole with a base coat. Then, with a product called Rub and Buff, I randomly added the product. Remember, a little goes a long way -- start with a tiny amount.

- No need for brushes; you can use your finger or a cloth.
- It is easily removed from your fingers with nail polish remover or mineral spirits.
- Play around with colors. It comes in nine different metallic finishes, from silver leaf to copper.
- The more you buff the finish, the shinier it will get!

Photo by Linda Wilson

My bamboo curtain rod came out exactly as I visualized it. Now, the question was how to hang it. After measuring the distance required from the wall to the vertical blinds, I knew I had to be creative again. Wandering through the big box store, I saw plant hangers. They would be the perfect size, so I purchased four of them. That project was now completed. Now to get material to make my curtains. Once each year, another big box store sells fabric for $1 per yard. I knew I needed curtain fabric, reupholstering material for the dining room chairs, which we already had, but the color was not complimentary, and valances and cornice board material. With spending a little less than $100, my mission was accomplished. Always look for sales or discontinued items or items that might be considered ugly. You can always make it to your liking.

Helping Family Members

David flew to Connecticut, loading up a 20' U-Haul and drove my aunt to Venice. The day they arrived, all I saw was a U-Haul loaded with love bugs splashed on the front of the vehicle and two "Q-tips" (both had beautiful white hair) sitting in the front seat. Now, my dad and my aunt could spend more time together. What I did not know was anything about sibling rivalry. I soon found out, and on more than one occasion, I had to send one of them to their room. I would take Dad to the Senior Friendship Center, and soon he became ill. He ended up in a nearby assisted living facility, and I started to teach arts and crafts there once a week. He soon passed away.

My aunt became a handful, and unfortunately, I had to Baker Act her. The Baker Act allows for the temporary detention and examination of people showing evidence of mental illness and who are in danger of harming themselves or others. This was extremely hard for me, but I knew she needed help. Once she was released and feeling better, I placed her in an assisted living facility. This facility would eventually be a future workplace for me. One of my favorite memories of her at the senior living facility was when I called a group of retired police officers who rode Harley motorcycles. You see, in her younger days, she had her own Harley. That is where I got my love of riding motorcycles. I owned two Triumphs because I could not afford a Harley. One of the police officers picked up my aunt, who weighed 89 pounds and gently placed her on a Harley. She had a huge smile on her face, and I knew she was recalling her younger days and the love of her life. It was not long after that she also passed away. I began spending all my days cleaning our home.

Photos by Linda Wilson

CHAPTER 15

NEW STATE – NEW BEGINNINGS

Photography: Remembering What Mom Taught Me

David came home one day and said that the company was looking for a photographer and did I wanted to apply. I said why not? And so I applied and got the job. This brought me back to when my mom was a photographer and how she was able to learn to operate the different cameras she used. I would be responsible for taking photographs of all the different phases of the jobs the company was doing. After getting my Nikon camera and learning how to use it, I started to love what I was doing. I had already bought a wide-angle printer, so I was able to produce any photo they wanted with no additional expense to them. My assignments varied from photographing marina resorts to hair salons to churches and synagogues, to senior living facilities, etc.

My most memorable photographs were as follows: Grand Riviera Condos on Golden Gate Point is located at the southern end of Golden Gate at 420 Golden Gate Point. This unique private enclave is home to 13 luxury residences ranging in size from 2,651 to 5,837sq.ft. Grande Riviera was completed in 2005 and has a distinct Old World Mediterranean design. Grande Riviera owners enjoy breathtaking views of the waters of Sarasota Bay and the Gulf of Mexico. When I first showed up, all the interiors were in different stages of completion. So, each floor was photographed separately and then came the outside of the building. An operator of a 50-to-70-foot scissor lift, a.k.a. "Aerial Work Platform", was assigned to me to take me up the side of the building. This was a two-person lift, one to operate it and one to take a ride. After I was strapped in, the operator asked, "Are you afraid of heights?" Nothing I could do, for we were on our way up, but I replied, "Not sure, but you will be the first to know if I am or not." He laughed. Oh, I found out that I was not afraid of heights.

Photos by Linda Wilson

Looking at the two pictures, you will notice a boat in the water. The boat originally was not there in that location, so I went out into the water and moved it. Also, if you look at the top picture on the far right-hand side you will notice the blue dome shown above. That is how high I went up on the scissor lift.

Photos by Linda Wilson

Asolo Theater was next. It is one of the most beautiful theaters I have ever seen. Located inside the John and Mable Ringling Museum of Art, the Historic Asolo Theater has Italian roots. It was first constructed in 1798, and the castle of Caterina Cornaro was its earlier address. Before it was deconstructed in 1930, this beautiful theater hosted versatile performances by Italian artists. In 1949, the theater was acquired by the museum. And was carefully shipped from Italy to the United States. Resembling the shape of a crescent, its three tiers of seats were carefully restored to preserve the essence of this Italian gem. With a series of events occupying its calendar, the Historic Asolo Theater is the city's preferred location for aficionados of performing arts. I was told that each of the surrounding paintings or objects found in Italy had a GPS location of each of the objects and were placed exactly at their new location in Sarasota, Florida, but I cannot find any evidence to prove that it had GPS locations.

After working in photography for years, capturing the construction progress of various retirement communities, banks, schools, planetariums, theaters, and businesses, the economic downturn of 2008 hit hard. The demand for construction-related photography dried up, and both David and I received our layoff slips. It was a tough blow, but we were determined to adapt and move forward.

Uncertain Future – Another Career Choice

During this challenging time, we developed friendships with several couples in our neighborhood. One couple, Joe and Cleighton, owned Groundworks Property Management, Inc., and offered me a position as their office manager. I figured I was well-suited for the role. I had taken many secretarial courses and had a solid background in design and drafting, which meant I could read blueprints, and I was familiar with Florida's latest Code Enforcement Rules thanks to our recent experience building our home. I also consider myself a good communicator—an essential skill for managing a property. The responsibilities of a property office manager were varied but familiar:

- Laws and Regulations: I navigated local laws and regulations, helping to prevent legal issues that could arise from missteps.
- Local Presence for Out-of-Town Owners: I acted as the eyes and ears for property owners who were not local, addressing maintenance issues and operational concerns that needed immediate attention.

- Handling Maintenance Requests: From broken appliances to unwanted pests, I managed a range of maintenance requests, ensuring that tenants felt heard and issues were promptly resolved.
- Showing and Leasing Vacant Units: I attracted new tenants and managed lease renewals, highlighting the full potential of the properties.
- Collecting and Depositing Rent: I handled rent collection, managed delinquent payments, and, when necessary, dealt with evictions.

With my earlier experience in record-keeping and compliance with state requirements, I quickly settled into the role. But soon after, one of the Groundworks co-owners, Cleighton, became ill, and both he and Joe decided to leave the business. They both found employment at a senior living facility—Joe in sales and Cleighton in maintenance.

Joe was particularly fond of our home and my decorating style. He asked if I would be interested in redecorating their two model apartments. I jumped at the opportunity, thrilled to dive back into my passion for decorating. After finishing the two model apartments, Joe asked if I could take photographs of the facility for use on promotional items like mouse pads and coasters. I agreed, and we spent a day capturing images from various vantage points, including the rooftop. I remember Joe holding onto my belt as I leaned over the edge to get the perfect shot. *Do not let me go*, I told him. He did not, and the job was completed without a hitch.

After the success of the model apartments and the promotional items, I was approached to spearhead a fundraising project for the community. We created the *"Aston Gardens Recipes & Remembrances Cookbook."* I designed a submission form where residents could contribute their recipes, dedicating them to loved ones. I researched software to compile and format the cookbook, ensuring it was professional and easy to navigate. The cookbook was a huge success and even went into a second printing. One of the most memorable submissions was a 90+-year-old woman's recipe for a peanut butter and jelly sandwich—simple yet full of heart. Many of the other recipes had been passed down through generations, preserving family traditions for the community to enjoy.

Photo by Linda Wilson

CHAPTER 16

THE VENICE FARMER'S MARKET

Farmer's Market Success Journey

While I was working on these projects, I met a woman, Nancy, who managed the local farmer's market. She was planning a vacation to Panama and asked if I could manage the market in her absence. How hard could it be, I thought. All it seemed to involve was collecting monthly fees from the vendors and making deposits. But as the summer season ended and winter approached, the vendor count began to grow, and so did my responsibilities. When the market manager returned after many months of vacationing, the City of Venice called both of us in for a meeting. The interim city manager explained that the market seemed to be having issues with growing in their current location. The city knew I had been collecting rent, organizing events, and setting up the market. This is Nancy Woodley's statement italicized:

"This was around 2008; I, Nancy Woodley, was interim city manager because Marty Black had retired, and the council was in a nationwide hunt for a replacement. The farmer's market was having some problems with participants leaving and no one person was in charge to respond with Nancy in Panama. (The city did not realize that during the summer months, some vendors would go back up north, decreasing vendor count, and during the winter months, the vendors would return, and vendor count would increase.) *The Council approved her* (Linda Wilson) *temporary appointment to help improve the management of the market. I remember that the manager's position was subsequently advertised as required by law, and you were*

the most qualified applicant, which resulted in her (Linda Wilson) *managing the market for many years thereafter."*

I read the city's rules and regulations meticulously, realizing that there was much work to be done. I distributed the contract to all current vendors and began making changes. The market was initially started in Centennial Park, in the center of town. While it was a picturesque setting, it became clear that we needed more space as the vendor count increased.

I visited local brick-and-mortar shop owners to discuss the possibility of moving the market. Most stores did not open until 9 or 10 a.m., so I explained that my job was to bring people downtown. After spending an hour or so at the market, customers would be encouraged to explore the local shops. The overwhelming support from Venice Main Street, the Venice Downtown Merchants Association, and the Venice Area Chamber of Commerce gave me the confidence to move forward with a new plan. We moved the market to Tampa Avenue, a street that paralleled the park. The new location was ideal, with a wide street that allowed for ample space between vendors. I envisioned the market as more than just a place to buy fresh produce. I wanted it to support economic development, education, health, and wellbeing, offer a forum for non-profits, and foster community relationships. I was asked to join the Venice Main Street Board of Directors and the Chamber of Commerce, both of which were instrumental in supporting the market. On September 20, 2011, the Venice Area Chamber of Commerce Ambassadors Council honored us with a Ribbon Cutting Celebration. Chamber members, most of the City Council, and all the vendors attended. It was a proud moment.

Each week, we featured different entertainers who played from 9 a.m. to 12 p.m. in the offseason and from 9 a.m. to 1 p.m. during peak season. Parents danced with their children, couples swayed together, and some patrons simply danced alone, lost in the music. It was a joyous sight, and we were careful to follow the city's noise regulations, ensuring the music did not start too early or play too loudly. David and I would arrive at 5 a.m. every Saturday, collecting barriers from the city's maintenance building. David blocked off one end of the street, and I blocked the other. After the street was blocked to traffic, came the inspection of the street: removing any dead animals, sweeping the water and leaves away from any vendor space, and turning on electricity for vendors that needed it. Vendor arrival was at 6 am, with the vendors having double spaces such as produce vendors or various plants and herbs entering first. We had a smooth operation, and the community embraced the market as a beloved local tradition. As the sun rose, we watched our market come to life, filled with vendors, customers, and the vibrant energy of a community coming together. It became a cornerstone of the community, and I was proud to have played a part in its success.

However, not everything was smooth sailing. One day, I picked up the local newspaper, The Gondolier Sun, and saw the headline: *"Farmer's Market Fracas."* A local shop owner had filed a complaint with the city, claiming that some market vendors were selling items *similar* to those in her store. The complaint was disheartening, and she made her grievances known in a rather unpleasant manner. I reported the incident to the local authorities to avoid any direct confrontation. It took time, but I knew the key to resolving the situation was patience. Sometimes, when you are winning, it is best to keep quiet and let things unfold. Patience paid off, and we continued to grow and thrive.

The market flourished, becoming a vibrant hub for the community. It was more than just a place to buy fresh produce; it was a place where people connected, shared stories and celebrated the best of what our town had to offer. And every week, as the sun rose and the music played, I felt a deep sense of fulfillment, knowing that I had played a part in creating something truly special.

Photo by Linda Wilson

Once the market was set up and open for business at 8 am, I would walk the length of the street socializing with everyone. Remember the word networking. One day, I saw a young boy, around 6 years old, holding up a tomato. I walked over to him and asked him where it came from. He thought for a moment and named a well-known local supermarket. I then asked where the supermarket got the tomato. His face went blank, looked at his mom, and I knew that he did not know. I explained that all the produce he saw came from various farms. He still had that blank look on his face. I knew then I was living in the city, and these kids did not know anything about farming. That week, I produced a new venue called The Kids Korner. I got on the phone and called the University of Florida Agricultural Department and asked if they wanted to have a booth for free at the market. A booth was set up each week, and the Master Gardeners came to educate people on how to grow fruits and vegetables, analyze their struggling plants, and take lessons in hydroponics vs. planting plants in soil. At The Kids Korner, we showed children how to plant vegetables in a 5-gallon bucket. Located behind the market was a senior living facility. We invited residents to work with kids, and everyone received their portable container vegetable garden. The Kids Korner also featured having the Boy Scouts teach the kids how to make survival bracelets, a local karate trainer giving beginning lessons in karate and several schools that had acting classes to perform original short plays. Elementary and high school' choirs came to perform. I contacted the Sarasota Chamber of Commerce as I learned they had started a program for young teens wanting to start businesses. I met a 13-year-old girl who made culinary confections. She brought me her resume, and because this was classified as a cottage food industry, it was my responsibility to inspect her home. All products used must be found in a separate area away from your cupboards or pantry areas, and if items are baked, that area would also have to be separated. Her other choice was to work in a commercial kitchen, but that would be too expensive. She was interviewed as any other vendor would have been. Her mother set up a separate area for her daughter to continue her dream. She developed quite a following.

I designed a Scavenger Hunt to have a parent and their child take part in a fun-loving, educational activity. I invited the Venice Police Department to instruct the children about "stranger danger" and what they should do if someone they did not know approached them. We had the Venice Fire Department teach them what they should do if they ever caught themselves on fire, the "stop-drop-roll" technique. School was just around the corner, so I sent an invitation to the Sarasota County Schools to learn proper etiquette while riding on a school bus. They were each given a detailed map of each of the scavenger items to be found, along with a rhyme associated with the item. Once they found the item, the vendor manning the booth would sign off on their paper. This promoted not only items at the market for the adults who may not have known of that vendor but also allowed parents and children to do something fun together. After the first hunt, the awards were handed out, one young couple came up to me and said, *"You do realize that some of these children don't know how to read yet."* A light bulb went on. Not having children, I realized that I would, the following year, put in photographs of the item they were searching for along with the rhyme to have them find the item. For the next five years, we had the Scavenger Hunt for Kids.

Photo by Linda Wilson

Introduction to SNAP, F.O.G., and Food Deserts

As I continued to walk the market, I realized that some vendors' money boxes were left out in the open. Times were tough, and we had people who were homeless or lived in areas that were called "food deserts." Could I lift their money boxes without the vendors knowledge? Yes! After I did, I stood back and watched their faces in shock, looking everywhere for their money boxes. I did not let them suffer for long, and soon, vendors started to take better care of their areas and hide their money boxes. Could this be my next career move as a thief? No, No, a Thousand Times.

I was becoming more aware of food deserts in our area. Food deserts are areas where people have limited access to a variety of healthy foods. This may be due to having a limited income or living far away from sources of healthful and affordable food. Now that I have a clear vision of what I saw as a farmers' market, how do I get the word out that we are more than a place selling produce and plants? I reserved the Chamber of Commerce's large conference room; I sent invitations to influential members of the community and invited all the vendors both in our town and the adjoining market in another town. The mayor, sitting council members, president of the Gulf Coast Community Foundation, Salvation Army, representatives of the Senior Friendship Center, Catholic Charities, Our Mothers House, and the local newspaper included it. I partnered with Sarasota County Area Transport (SCAT), and they offered a monthly free pass to those on SNAP.

I needed to do something. I applied to the SNAP (aka Food Stamps) Program for the market through the Florida Growers Association and received a grant. If the vendor qualified to be a SNAP participant, they were given signs to be displayed at their tents notifying customers that they could shop there. Reaching out and interacting with SNAP recipients has been an extreme pleasure, and they are extremely grateful that such a program exists. I have been told that it is hard enough for the working person to acknowledge that they are on a SNAP, but it has been a lifesaver for them to have this great benefit. All Faiths Food Bank also partnered with us to help us get the word out and hand out literature for the Venice Farmer's

Market (VFM). Numerous articles about the SNAP & FAB program were featured in our local newspaper, and we posted flyers at locations such as Salvation Army and Our Mother's House at Epiphany Cathedral Church. We also shared information at the local hospital and on our Facebook page. Slowly but surely, the word spread, and each week, we welcomed new customers to the market.

I am not a 501C3 organization, and getting the word out was a challenge as I was the only one who managed the market with aid from my husband. I was hoping to get the information to our schools for their Backpack Program but could not because of my for-profit standing. Customers went to the Management Booth, where they would present their SNAP cards and receive tokens to buy products. They would shop, give the vendor their tokens, and at the end of the day, each vendor would return their coins to the Management Booth. The following week each vendor would receive a check for the number of tokens they collected the previous week. It was going very well. Monthly, I selected a non-profit organization that helps our residents in our community and gives them a free space at the market to share their information with the public.

However, not being a SNAP recipient myself, I reached out to Karen, a volunteer assisting with SNAP benefits at the market, who was. This Is her statement: *"I think Churches are an excellent support system for recipients of SNAP. However, there is still a lot of prejudice against those who receive SNAP benefits and those who do not. I have a list of Churches that offer free food to the "hungry. The problem is that many of the people in need are not hungry but have a need to supplement their "food basket" because of external stresses on their budget.*

The faces of the SNAP program have changed as well as the increasing numbers of recipients. Sensitivity is an issue and privacy is a concern. In the past, "those" people receiving benefits were from non-working or homeless groups, but now, "those" people may be working family members, neighbors, homeowners, retirees, or others with financial stress or budget strains due to increased taxes, insurance, medical, reduction of hours on their job, and the list goes on. Bringing awareness regarding "who" we are reaching out to and why is especially important. Our focus should be centered on a healthy choice of fresh products at a "price" that is within reach of everyone regardless of "income" is essential. We are not targeting "groups", and we are redefining "need." I continued to work with this SNAP recipient to better focus on redefining the "need" through food demonstrations at the market, advertising the "In Season" produce at the market and on our Facebook page, and placing recipes on our website: www.venicefarmersmkt@gmail.com.

Market shoppers initially struggled to find vendors participating in the SNAP program, so I implemented a simple yet effective solution using color-coded plastic plates that matched their tokens. Each vendor with eligible items displayed a specific-colored plate that corresponded to the SNAP tokens they accepted. Customers were given a coordinating sheet explaining what each of the three colors represented, making it easy to find vendors who accepted SNAP benefits. At participating booths, all produce was labeled with matching colored sticker dots, aligning with the colored plates and the document outlining eligible SNAP items. Eligible food items included:

- Fruits and vegetables
- Meat, poultry, and fish
- Dairy products
- Breads and cereals
- Other foods like snack foods and non-alcoholic beverages

- Seeds and plants that produce food for the household

VFM supported a robust advertising plan with the Venice Gondolier, promoting our SNAP & FAB program. Fresh Access Bucks (FAB) is a nutrition incentive program that doubles the purchasing power of SNAP recipients for fresh fruits and vegetables at farmer's markets, produce stands, mobile markets, community grocery outlets and Community Supported Agriculture (CSAs). CSA is a system where consumers support local farms by subscribing to receive regular deliveries of fresh produce and other farm products. For example, a SNAP cardholder who spends $10 off their benefits receives an added $10 to purchase more fresh, local produce. This not only increased revenues for Florida farmers and distributors but also made healthy, fresh fruits and vegetables more accessible to low-income families.

We continued to promote SNAP & FAB on Facebook and partnered with the University of Florida/Institute of Florida Agriculture Services (UF/IFAS) Family Nutrition Program to provide educational sessions on healthy eating and lifestyles. The UF/IFAS Master Gardeners also joined us, teaching attendees how to grow their own fresh fruits and vegetables. I further engaged with LOVN CHAT (Laurel Osprey, Venice, Nokomis Community Health Action Team) to strengthen community relationships and spread the word.

The VFM secured various funding sources for these initiatives, including a one-year advertising deal with the Gondolier Sun Newspaper valued at $6,432. Vendor Suzanne contributed $30 per month for nine months to perform food demonstrations using produce bought from VFM vendors. We also organized Strawberry, Peach, and Mango Tasting Events, collaborating with UF/IFAS to gather consumer preferences and inform Florida farmers about the most popular varieties. This event cost $300, funded by the Venice Farmer's Market.

At the end of each market week, I sent detailed reports for SNAP compliance. I knew site visits from Florida Organic Growers (FOG) were possible, though unannounced. This encouraged us to support rigorous standards, ensuring all produce came from organic farms, proudly displayed at the vendors' booths. Our partnership with FOG was a natural fit, reflecting our commitment to providing high-quality, locally grown produce.

Photo by: Linda Wilson

One day, while wrapping up the market, I noticed a vendor flipping SNAP tokens and heading to the Manager's booth to redeem them. As I passed by, he jokingly said, "You didn't see that," and walked away. I knew what items he sold, and none were SNAP-eligible. Unacceptable SNAP items include:

- Beer, wine, liquor, cigarettes, or tobacco

- Vitamins, medicines, and supplements

- Live animals (except shellfish, fish removed from the water, and animals slaughtered before pick-up)

- Foods that are hot at the point of sale

- Any non-food items such as pet food, cleaning supplies, paper products, household supplies, hygiene items, and cosmetics

For the next month, I carefully checked the distribution and redemption of tokens. The discrepancy was staggering. I discovered that some vendors were collecting tokens for ineligible items, undermining the integrity of the program. I reported my findings to my FOG manager, who asked how I wanted to handle the situation. I decided to address it directly with the vendors, believing everyone deserved a second chance. The following Saturday, I called a meeting with all the vendors and explained what I had found. I outlined how I had found fraud and made it clear that such behavior would not be tolerated. I warned the vendors that any continuation of these actions would result in immediate expulsion from the market and a permanent ban from taking part in any market offering SNAP benefits. I did not name names, but after the meeting, several vendors approached me, confessing their involvement and promising it would never happen again. My FOG manager informed the manager of another market about the situation, knowing that it existed in his market, and he expressed gratitude for my approach in handling it without resorting to harsh penalties.

Contests, Fundraisers and Awards

With the issue resolved, I set my sights on more positive goals. In 2011, the American Farmland Trust held a contest to decide the best farmer's market in each state. I decided to throw our hat in the ring. In November, we received a letter along with a certificate letting us know that the Venice Farmer's Market was ranked number one in Florida. It was a tremendous honor and validation of all our hard work. Winning this award reignited my passion for excellence. I believed in the entrepreneurial ethos that hard work, perseverance, and dedication could overcome seemingly impossible challenges. This mindset drove me to pursue more awards and recognition for our market. In 2013, we received a letter from the local newspaper informing us that we were in the running for the Gondolier Sun "Best of Venice" Readers' Choice Award in the Produce category. We won first place that year and, for the next four years, placed in the Finalist Category (2nd Place) as the competition grew, but the recognition was still deeply satisfying.

2013 also brought an opportunity to give back to our community through a fundraiser for the local police department. After speaking with various law enforcement departments, I learned that many had Segways to patrol downtown areas, during parades, and on the beaches. I applied for a permit to hold a fundraiser in Centennial Park. We roped off an area, and a Segway owner volunteered to teach patrons how to ride. Our fundraising committee included a local bank representative, several downtown merchants, a member of the Venice Police Department, and me. It was a huge success, raising funds to support our local law enforcement and fostering a stronger sense of community. One of the board members was a vice president at a local bank, and the funds we raised for the police department went into a dedicated account. In just six months, we managed to raise $13,000, which we used to buy the department's first Segway and taser. To celebrate this achievement, we hosted a Great Gatsby-themed party, inviting everyone who contributed to the cause. I will never forget the moment when our Police Chief rode the Segway onto the dance floor, showing just how easily it maneuvered through the crowd. It was a joyful reminder of what a community can carry out when it comes together for a common goal. In 2014, I was honored to receive the Top 40 Business Professionals Award. It was a testament to the hard work and dedication I put into the farmer's market and other community projects.

Photo by Linda Wilson

The Venice Farmer's Market: A Beacon of Economic and Social Impact

After years of nurturing the Venice Farmer's Market, in May 2015, an opportunity arose that would highlight the market's true value. MarketUmbrella.org, in collaboration with students from Loyola University, selected our market for an evaluation to measure its economic impact on the community. I knew this would provide the statistics the Venice Economic Development Advisory Board had long been seeking. Loyola University's Economics Institute employed the Sticky Economic Evaluation Device (SEED) method, a comprehensive tool that measured not only the money spent at the market but also the ripple effect on surrounding businesses and vendor spending. When the results were in, I was over the moon: the Venice Farmer's Market was bringing nearly $15.9 million annually into the city. This revelation validated our efforts and underscored the market's role as a cornerstone of the local economy.

In 2017, I was notified that I was in the running for the Visit Sarasota County Guest Service Excellence Award in Management. I did not know who had nominated me, but I was thrilled to be considered. I was up against 11 other candidates in Sarasota County, all outstanding in their fields. I was standing at the edge of the stage, holding my breath, when the winner was announced. As my name was called, all the other candidates rushed up to congratulate me. I was in such disbelief that I almost fell off the stage! It was an incredible honor, and I felt deeply grateful for the recognition. This moment of recognition was not just a personal victory; it was a celebration of the community I had worked so hard to support.

As the saying goes, "If you love what you do, you'll never have to work a day in your life." David and I spent countless hours brainstorming new and fun ideas for the vendors and our patrons. For example, February in Florida is strawberry season. In my weekly email to all vendors, I proposed a strawberry-themed challenge. Whether they sold food or crafts, I encouraged them to incorporate strawberries into their offerings. I invited three Council members to judge the entries and awarded two prizes. Everyone participated, and it was a huge hit!

We also collaborated with Venice Main Street to host an Oktoberfest celebration. Venice Main Street obtained a liquor permit, and I found a performer who played the Swiss Alp Horn while dressed in traditional lederhosen. I wore a dirndl, the traditional dress for women in southern Germany and the Alpine regions. The money we raised paid the liquor vendors, and the remaining funds were donated to a local non-profit organization.

A Difficult Decision: Confronting Change Amidst Personal Struggles

However, in the late spring of 2017, I was called into the mayor's office. He informed me that he wanted to move the farmers' market from its current location to the parking lot at City Hall. I was caught off guard and asked him why this sudden change was necessary, but he did not give a clear answer. I requested time to compile a Pro vs Con list about the move and present it to the City Council in two weeks. When I completed the list, the pros of staying in our current location far outweighed the cons. Our location provided easy access for emergency vehicles to reach the assisted living facility or the KMI building, which housed shops and condominiums. Downtown merchants supported us because they benefited from the increased foot traffic, and the market vendors did not take up any space in Centennial Park while it was open. Most of the vendors attended the Council meeting in support. When it was my turn to speak, I presented the data and the benefits of staying in our current location. Despite my efforts, I could sense the decision had already been made. After several Council members asked questions, they voted to move the market. I was devastated. As I stood up to leave, I turned back to the Council and said, "Mr. Mayor and Council Members, I would like to give you my resignation effective June 30, 2017." They seemed taken aback and reminded me that my contract with the City was valid until the end of the calendar year. I responded, "If you read the contract closely, you'll see I can give a 30-day notice."

I will never forget the headline in our local newspaper: "Farmer's Market Savior, Leader to Retire!" I never thought of myself that way because I genuinely loved what I was doing. Is it fate or fortune that decides our future? It is a brain-twisting question that almost everyone ponders at some point. If everything is preordained by fate, why work hard? But the truth is, our destiny is shaped by our hard work, perseverance, and the choices we make.

A few weeks earlier, prior to handing in my resignation, I had experienced sharp, sudden pains in my left side. Concerned, I visited my doctor, who at once sent me to the hospital for tests. I was admitted, and after a series of tests, the family physician, whom I call my guardian angel, informed me that I had kidney cancer and scheduled the operation for the following day.

A Personal Battle: Confronting Health Challenges

At the time, I was still recovering from surgery that had removed most of my cancerous kidney. I did not want David to bear the burden of the market's responsibilities, but I knew I needed to focus on healing. I remember being wheeled into the operating room and then nothing. When I woke up, David told me that they had put me into an induced coma to aid in my recovery. While a coma can be a terrifying experience, under the right circumstances, it can be lifesaving. At one point, I felt as though I was floating above myself, watching the scene unfold. I saw David alone, crying, pounding on the end of the hospital bed, saying, "No, you cannot leave me! Honey, I do not know how to do laundry or turn the dishwasher on!" When I finally came out of the coma seven days later, I asked David if he had said and done what I thought I had seen. He confirmed it. I realized then that I could not leave him. There was still so much more to do. I was not finished here on earth.

With that clarity, after I reminded the Council of my 30-day notice, they accepted my resignation. I offered to help with the search for a new market manager, knowing how crucial it was to find the right person for the role. I took part in all the interviews, offering my insights and recommendations. At the end of June 2017, the vendors threw me a farewell party and gave me a card that I cherish to this day. Out of the 34 summer vendors, eight went on to open brick-and-mortar stores while continuing to sell at the market. Seeing them achieve this dream was incredibly rewarding, as one of my goals when I took over the market was to help vendors transition into permanent retail spaces.

After the City of Venice selected a new manager for the farmers' market, I was saddened to see many of the programs I had started, like the Kids Korner, non-profit organizations, and the scavenger hunt, were discontinued.

One day, I received a call from the regional leader of the Girl Scouts of America. It was a cookie-selling season, but the scouts were told they would have to pay for a booth. She asked if I could help, but I explained that I no longer had any influence over market operations. It became increasingly uncomfortable for me to visit the market. Every time I went to see my former vendors, I was followed by one of the current managers or comanagers. I was not trying to start my own market; I just wanted to support the vendors I had grown close to.

Five years later, I returned to the market under new management again. Most of my vendors had left for various reasons, but those who remained told me, "We miss you!" The market now has many food trucks and many vendors offering similar products. It was a different market with new rules and a new atmosphere.

The Power of Lifelong Learning and Adaptability

My story is not just about career progression; it is about the power of lifelong learning and adaptability. I never let the lack of formal education define what I could or could not do. Instead, I focused on acquiring knowledge, whether through hands-on experience, self-study, or learning from others. I built a diverse skill set that allowed me to navigate different fields and roles with confidence. Each transition, whether from secretary to draftsman, manager, decorator, or volunteer, was fueled by curiosity, hard work, and a belief that learning is a continuous, self-driven process. I embraced every opportunity to grow, no matter how unconventional the path.

Reflection

I am living proof that formal education, while valuable, is not the only path to success. With passion, perseverance, and an unyielding commitment to self-improvement, it is possible to achieve your dreams and even surpass them. My career has been a journey of self-discovery, continuous learning, and the courage to take chances. If you can imagine it, you can do it. All it takes is action on your part.

CHAPTER 17

LIFE IN A POLICE DEPARTMENT

Volunteering in Cold Cases

Not long after leaving the market, I received a call from the Venice Police Department Chief, asking if I would be interested in volunteering. Little did I know that my time with the Venice Police Department would present me with opportunities I never imagined. My organizational skills and experience with project management made me an asset, and I was soon involved in cold case work forensic evidence management and even played a role in designing their new facility. I did not need a background in law enforcement; I needed a willingness to learn and a drive to contribute meaningfully.

I was honored when the Chief asked me to volunteer. David and I had just completed the first Citizens Police Academy training, during which we underwent extensive background checks, passing with flying colors. After my orientation and testing, I was officially accepted as a volunteer. I was then escorted to the Detective's Division, where I was introduced to my new team members. To my surprise, the three people who joined me were all former NSA (National Security Agency) employees from Fort G. Meade, Maryland. The NSA is known for its role in producing and managing information assurance and signals intelligence (SIGINT) for the U.S. government. Their work involves global monitoring, collection, decoding, and subsequent analysis and translation of information and data for foreign intelligence and counter-intelligence purposes.

I could not help but wonder what I, a community volunteer, could possibly offer alongside such highly educated and experienced individuals. They quickly explained that they needed someone to look at an old case with fresh eyes to organize the files that had been sitting in two large boxes for 22 years. It was a cold case that had recently been reopened, and they believed a new perspective could shed new light on the evidence. This was something I excelled at: organizing, sorting, and finding patterns. So, I got to work.

The boxes were filled with a mix of small torn pieces of paper, 8.5 inches by 11 inches sheets, and casual note-sized scraps, each holding bits of information. I read every single piece, sorted them, and began to create a comprehensive timeline of events. It was meticulous work, but I felt a sense of purpose in piecing together the puzzle. Due to the case's sensitive nature, we collaborated closely with the FBI and the State Attorney General. I was tasked with developing a presentation for them, outlining our findings and proposing the next steps. Of course, my associates reviewed it before the meeting. The presentation went well, and we gained their support in our continued investigation.

Our volunteer team requested to visit the crime scene better to understand the layout and context of the events. The Captain drove us to the location, and despite some changes over the years, the essential layout stayed the same. We had a video from an adjacent car wash showing the suspect walking beside the house on the night of the crime. Unfortunately, the individual wore a hoodie and kept their face turned away from view, making identification impossible. The only possible clue that could be inferred was the person's gait, which suggested they were possibly middle-aged.

As I continued organizing the evidence, I created another sorting list based on the value of each piece of evidence. The integrity of evidence is crucial in court, so we had to ensure it was properly collected, preserved, and analyzed. The Forensic Team guided us through the evidence room, showing items ranging from refrigerated samples to tangible objects sealed in bags. Everything matched the department's computer list of collected evidence, but we were not allowed to handle it directly. The following information was what I gathered by taking notes and going to a seminar in Tampa, Florida.

Medical Examination Evidence:

Hair (both pubic and head hair):

- It cannot conclusively identify an individual unless the root is intact.
- Provides strong supporting evidence if the individual was present at the crime scene.
- It can differentiate between human and animal hair and sometimes determine race or the area of the body the hair originated from.

Fibers:

- Due to mass production, fibers have limited value for individual identification.
- In rare instances, fibers can provide strong evidence for individual identification.

Blood:

- Can distinguish between human and animal blood.
- DNA analysis can be used to identify an individual.

Fingernail Scrapings:

- Collects DNA evidence that can be used for individual identification.

- Vaginal, Rectal, and Oral Swabs:
- These swabs are used to collect DNA evidence for individual identification.

Objectives:

1. Identify, document, and collect evidence of the events that took place.
2. Establish a connection between the victim, suspect, and the crime scene.
3. Identify and locate any witnesses.
4. Apprehend the individual(s) responsible for the crime.

Survivors Accounts:

The survivors had been attacked from behind, one at her home after returning from work and the other on the beach at night in a town further north of Venice, so they had little information regarding the suspect's description. Despite following protocol, which included providing this information to patrol units, the case soon went cold and remained unsolved for 22 years—until it was resurrected. During my time with the department, I was unexpectedly sent to Tampa for training. Although I was not originally scheduled to attend, I took the place of a teammate who could not go. As a result, all the training certificates ended up in her name. The seminar was a unique experience, bringing together people from across the country-sheriffs, police captains, and DNA experts-each contributing their expertise for a common cause.

Towards the end of the seminar, I was pulled out of class and informed that my brother's partner of 26 years, Joey, had passed away suddenly in his sleep. They had only been married for four months before Joey's untimely death. It was another devastating loss for me, and David was already on his way to pick me up. It was the middle of December, and snow covered the ground in Georgia, but nothing was going to stop us from reaching my brother. When we arrived, he was surrounded by his closest friends and neighbors, but after a while, everyone left, and he was alone with his grief. We stayed for a week, trying to help in any way we could-visiting the crematorium with him, cooking meals that could be frozen for later, and just being there to support him. He finally said he needed some time alone to process everything, and we made our way back home. I still regret not staying longer or being more supportive during that difficult time.

Once I returned home from Georgia, I resumed my volunteering at the Venice Police Department. Shortly afterward, we received word that our detectives were on their way to Ohio to apprehend the suspect in the 22 Year Cold Case file. His DNA was a perfect match to the evidence we had on file. He was brought back to the Sarasota County Jail, but six months later, he passed away. I was relieved that the two survivors of the assault would not have to relive their trauma by testifying in court. Justice had been served in a way that spared them further pain.

Shortly after, I was asked if I would like to be transferred to the Forensics Department. I eagerly accepted. I was welcomed by two women, Cheryl and Tawnie, who worked in the department, and we were tasked with eliminating evidence in cases that had already been closed. My role included communicating with the state attorney to get permission to destroy evidence, and I enjoyed learning something new in this field. One day, I was invited to visit the facility where all the evidence was destroyed. It was an eye-opening experience, bringing me full circle in understanding the entire lifecycle of a criminal case.

Uninspected Opportunities: How a Pandemic Shifted My Purpose

In addition, COVID-19 made its way to Venice and prevented me from working in person with the forensics team. Just when I thought my volunteering days might be over, I received a call from our new chief of police asking if I could utilize my decorating skills. A new police station was being built less than a mile away from the current facility, and they needed someone to help with the interior design. I jumped at the opportunity to shift my priorities back to commercial decorating. Once the walls, drywall, and painting were complete, the chief invited me to walk through the building with the contractors. I designed the logo for the community room, built a historical display of the Venice Police Department in collaboration with the Venice Area Historical Society, arranged photos of all the Citizens Police Department graduates, and dedicated a wall to honor all former police chiefs. One of my proudest moments was when I asked an officer to pose for a photograph in the men's locker room. I had him sit on a bench with his head down, and above the image, I wrote, "The Devil Saw Me With My Head Down And Thought He'd Won, Until I Said, AMEN." These words came from our Chief, and I thought it would be appropriate to place them on top of the photograph. The photograph and verbiage captured the strength and resilience of our officers in a way that was both powerful and deeply meaningful. The grand opening of the new police station was a success, and by then, they had hired a new person for the Forensics Department, leaving me without a role once again.

Photo by Linda Wilson

Meanwhile, life outside of volunteering was challenging. After several years of marriage and having her son, Molly had an affair. Her husband caught them, and a confrontation ensued. They divorced, and she soon married the man she had an affair with. Molly had a great job at American Express, and we would talk every Monday, sharing stories and learning new management skills together.

CHAPTER 18

FIGHTING FOR LIFE

Three Heartbreaking Choices: A Dog's Life Hanging in the Balance

One Monday morning, I called Molly, and I knew something was wrong. She soon burst into tears. She told me that while playing with one of their dogs, Ricki, the dog yelped and could not get up. They rushed Ricki to the vet, who referred them to a specialist. The specialist presented them with three options:

1. Operate on Ricki with no guarantees of success.
2. Put Ricki in a sling to support her back legs.
3. Euthanize Ricki.

They went home to think it over. This is what I call a "Timing Call." I immediately told Molly that David and I would come to get Ricki. She was worried about what her dad would say, but I assured her he would agree. We left immediately, picked up Ricki, and brought her back to our home.

I began researching hydrotherapy or aquatic therapy for dogs in our area. Fortunately, I found the perfect facility in Sarasota, though they have since relocated to Tampa. Timing is everything, as I have often said. Hydrotherapy, also known as aquatic therapy, is a form of physical therapy for dogs that utilizes the buoyancy of water. A certified hydro therapist leads the dog through exercises in water at a specially equipped rehabilitation center. This low-impact treatment helps improve strength, range of motion, and endurance. The buoyancy of water minimizes weight-bearing stress on the joints, preventing tissue injuries, inflammation, and pain.

Conditions Aquatic Therapy Can Help Treat:

- Pain due to hip dysplasia
- Metabolic conditions such as Cushing's and diabetes, which can result in muscle atrophy
- Paralysis in dogs

The underwater treadmill, a key component of this therapy, allows for controlled weightbearing exercises by varying the water level. Ricki was introduced to this, and I was allowed to enter the tank with her to offer assistance if needed.

Gradually, Ricki began to walk on the treadmill as the water's resistance provided strength training without the stress of gravity. At home, I used a TENS unit on Ricki for 15-20 minutes a day. The TENS machine stimulates nerves in the affected area, encouraging muscle contraction and relaxation, which is particularly beneficial for dogs suffering from muscle atrophy due to inactivity or injury.

For the next three weeks, I slept on the lanai with Ricki, using a makeshift sling to support her hindquarters when she needed to go outside. Slowly but surely, Ricki regained her strength. After four weeks, she was running again. Her mom and dad came to pick her up, and she lived pain-free for another three years until she passed away.

CHAPTER 19

DAVID'S JOURNEY: SURGERY, SURVIVAL, EMOTIONAL TRAUMA, & SETBACKS

Our 35th wedding anniversary fell on November 26th, 2020, the day after Thanksgiving, as David had planned all those years ago so he would always remember. We went out to dinner to celebrate. When the waitress asked what we wanted to drink, I ordered wine, and David asked for a Coke. A Coke? This was not like him at all; he usually ordered a Bloody Mary. Something was seriously wrong. The following day, I asked him to get on the scale and discovered he had lost twenty pounds. At 6-foot 1 inch, he normally weighed around 175 to 180 pounds, but now he was down to 160. I did not hesitate. I insisted he get into the car, and we headed to the hospital. I knew he was unwell because he would never agree to see a doctor or go to the hospital unless the pain was unbearable.

He was admitted, and on December 14th, 2020, he underwent surgery to remove 2 feet of his colon and intestines, along with a 2.5-inch tumor. I visited him daily, and soon he was back home. We soon learned that his claim for $5,124.00 was denied by the hospital because it was out of network. We were stunned and frustrated, having not been informed of this before the surgery. Despite the financial stress, we focused on his recovery. It soon became clear that we needed to explore other treatment options as David's abdominal pain was intensifying. I gathered his daughter, Molly, and our son-in-law to discuss possible paths forward. I put together a chart outlining various treatment options for the family to consider, although it would ultimately be David's decision.

On January 11, 2021, we visited the Florida Cancer Specialists. The doctor reviewed all the information I had meticulously collected. When she finally entered the room, she stated bluntly, "I recommend chemotherapy and hospice." That was it. We stood up, walked out, and immediately requested a second opinion. On February 10, 2021, Florida Cancer Specialists scheduled us with a different doctor, but due to COVID-19 restrictions, I was not allowed to accompany David inside. Molly suggested we investigate the Cleveland Clinic, as her former husband's wife worked there and could help expedite the process. She arranged a phone consultation for February 8, 2021, and I sent all of David's medical records ahead of time. The call lasted an hour. They explained that he would need to make a three-hour trip to Cleveland Clinic for chemotherapy and then drive three hours back home. This grueling regime would last between 13 to 18 months—a daunting prospect.

While researching, I discovered that immunotherapy, a treatment aiming to boost the body's natural defenses to combat cancer, was first introduced in 1891 by Dr. William Coley. It had shown promise as a revolutionary approach to cancer treatment. On January 26, 2021, I had a conversation with a doctor from Chipsa Hospital in Mexico, which specialized in immunotherapy. He explained their protocol thoroughly and connected us with other patients who had undergone similar treatments. What appealed to David most was that their treatment would only last three weeks, not the 13 to 18 months required by traditional methods. Before making a final decision, David arranged another appointment with Florida Cancer Specialists to ensure they would continue his care upon his return from Mexico. The doctor agreed and even set up an appointment for four days after we returned. David felt hopeful and asked me to make the necessary reservations for the trip to Mexico. He was drawn to the long history of immunotherapy in Mexico, the condensed treatment timeline, and the fact that we would be staying in a condominium where I could be with him, although not during his treatments.

We gathered the family to share David's decision. His daughter was not happy and expressed her concerns, believing I had influenced his choice. But this was David's decision, and off we went to Mexico, where he began treatments immediately. Each day, David would return with updates from his treatments, which I would translate from Spanish to English. Using WhatsApp, I relayed these updates to everyone following our journey. The results after three weeks were astonishing. His tumors were decreasing in size or gone completely. As we left Mexico, we were escorted back to the U.S. with a supply of medications for David to continue his treatment at home. We returned on a Saturday, hopeful and relieved.

The following Wednesday, we went back to Florida Cancer Specialists. I still was not allowed inside due to COVID-19 protocols. Eventually, the doctor came out to speak with me. I tried to hand him the documentation from David's doctors in Mexico detailing the dramatic reduction in tumor size, but he refused to even look at it. "I can't treat him," he said dismissively. "I'm not going to acknowledge these recommendations." I was in shock. David emerged from the appointment, silent and visibly shaken. As we walked to the car, he finally said, "It was like a gut punch. I am done."

From that moment, we knew we were on our own. Friends came by to talk privately with David, and to this day, I do not know what they discussed, but I am grateful they had that time with him. For the next six weeks, I administered the medications from Chipsa Hospital diligently. I monitored his blood pressure, charted his progress, and reported it to Hospice daily. His medications needed to be taken every three hours, around the clock, and somehow, I always woke up on time to give them to him.

On May 5, 2021, I gave him his meds at 4:15 a.m. and then fell asleep beside him. I awoke suddenly at 4:30 a.m. and realized David had passed away. This was, and still is, the most heartbreaking day of my life. Someone stated there is always something to be gained in times of loss, but I am still searching for what that might be for me. I know I will never have answers to all my questions, like "Why?"

We were married for 35 and a half years, and during that time, I fell in love with David repeatedly. But what is love, really? I have learned that it cannot be defined in a single word because life throws so many different challenges and obstacles our way. Love, I have discovered, is about accepting imperfections, respecting each other, staying committed, making sacrifices, understanding, upholding shared values, being honest, and working hard together. Love people while you can because there are no guarantees they will be there tomorrow. The future can be fearful or full of promise; it all depends on how you choose to see it. See people for who they are, not who you want them to be. Life is too short to settle. Love has no bounds, but the risk of love is loss.

I still remember how David would call me to him at 4:30 in the morning, put his hands caressing my face, tell me how much he loved me and then ask me "Honey, what's for dinner?" I remember the bear hugs he would give me and how he would tell me during COVID-19, "Honey, I have the perfect solution." He disappeared and then came back with a "Maxie Pad" wrapped around his face. His humor, his embrace, and his love for me are what I miss. One day, I asked what he was doing out on the lanai as the sun was beating down from behind, and he was standing there with his cell phone. His answer was, "I'm taking a selfie." His definition of a selfie was taking a picture of his shadow.

I called Molly and asked if she could accompany me to the funeral home to pick up David's ashes. The funeral director brought out a velvet-covered box, and Molly and I both held out our arms to accept it. It was a solemn and heartbreaking moment. At the end of June 2021, I discovered that I needed surgery. Molly called and offered to take me to the hospital, but she mentioned that several people at her workplace had contracted COVID. Even though she showed no symptoms, I worried she could be a carrier. I thanked her for her offer but told her I would find someone else to take me. Since then, I have not heard from her, which has been incredibly painful for me.

In December, I decided to change our will. I created a Trust Fund in our names, with the Gulf Coast Community Foundation to administer my wishes. Upon my passing, the sale of my home will go toward scholarships for seniors attending Venice High School entering the trades. Not everyone wants to attend college, and we need skilled tradespeople, plumbers, electricians, and drywall installers to keep building our communities. I believe David would have approved of this decision.

Months went by in a blur. I cannot recall what I did or whom I saw. It felt like I was in a fog, unable to see beyond my outstretched hand. I know friends visited because my kitchen counter was piled high with unfamiliar items. Though all of this, our best friends, Chetta and Larry, were there. I love you both!

Photo supplied

CHAPTER 20

FIRST STEP TO HEALING

Seven months later, I received a call from our friends Ralph and Joseph. During their private time with David, he had told them he hoped they could take me to Europe, something I had always wanted to do, though I had dreamed of going with David. Royal Caribbean was launching the maiden voyage of the Wonder of the Seas with a transatlantic cruise, and we were off. Leaving Miami, we sailed across the Atlantic with breathtaking sunrises and sunsets, friendly fellow passengers, delicious food, and fantastic entertainment. The three of us met every morning for breakfast and every evening for dinner, spending our days exploring the ship on our own.

Serendipity at Sea: A Bond Beyond Borders

One day, while attending a seminar at the spa, I found myself sitting next to a lovely German lady named Silki. We connected instantly as if we had known each other for years. From that moment on, I would join Silki and her husband, Tobi, at various shows after dinner. By the end of the cruise, Silki began calling me "her American mom," a title that touched my heart deeply. What started as a chance meeting blossomed into more than just friendship—it became family.

Photo by Linda Wilson

When we disembarked in Barcelona, Spain, we continued to Paris, England, and Italy. I was still in a fog, fumbling with my paperwork and passport and often becoming a nervous wreck. I am not a seasoned traveler, and I took my time to capture photos to remember where I had been. I know Ralph was frustrated with me, and later, once we returned home, he told me I was not the sharp, intelligent person he once knew. Grief has a way of changing everything in your life. When your spouse dies, everything changes. It affects your self-worth, your rhythms, and even the way you breathe and think. You become a new, different person, not by choice but by circumstance. I am sorry Ralph did not understand what I was going through. Grief is a journey with no set timeline, and it is different for everyone. It is only when you are ready that you can begin to heal.

We do not control the events in our lives, but we can control how we respond to them. When you start to understand this, you gain the power to shape your life. No one can choose your thoughts or actions but you. With awareness comes choice, and with choice comes empowerment.

There will always be things beyond our control - circumstances we are born into, natural disasters, pandemics, illness, job loss, accidents, and the death of loved ones. What we can control is how we think and feel about these events and how we respond. There are always people who thrive in times of crisis, not because they are lucky but because they choose to see opportunities instead of disadvantages.

Starting anew means taking stock of what you have done in your life. Have you taken courses that inspired you? Have you helped someone in a way that intrigued you or made you feel like you could make a difference? The more difficult your life has been, the harder it may seem to start over. But it is worth trying because it is your life, and no one else will be as invested in it as you are. Forever love is one of life's greatest achievements, and it comes with great risk. You come into the world with love, and you should go out with love.

CHAPTER 21

STEPPING UP: A JOURNEY OF LEADERSHIP, COMMUNITY, AND CONNECTION

Several months later, I received a call from my best friend, Chetta, about a job opportunity. I had known Chetta since 2013 when I moved the farmer's market to Tampa Avenue. She was working at an assisted living facility and was involved with a Bloodhound Search and Rescue Group, which I also supported. She told me the facility where she was currently working needed an assistant activities director. Eager to get back to work, I went for an interview.

The activities director explained my potential duties: teaching arts and crafts, going out to lunch with residents, taking notes during Resident Council meetings, and serving snacks and drinks at happy hour on Fridays. It was four days a week, and I agreed. Eventually, she asked if I could work weekends as well, but I explained I could only work Saturdays due to other commitments.

Soon after, the activities director had an accident and went on disability. She claimed a resident fell backward onto her, injuring her arm and hand. The company sent her to rehab and did everything possible to accommodate her. She still did not want to come back, and she eventually sued the company. I was approached to take over her duties and was promoted to active activities coordinator. My background in event planning, organizing fundraisers, and teaching arts and crafts made me a good fit for the role. I organized trips to interesting places around Venice, such as Clyde Butcher's Photography Studio and the Train Depot. I also organized two fundraisers: one for the Loveland Center, raising $600, and another for Venice Animal Rescue, raising $850, utilizing the many different arts and crafts projects the residents made.

Photo by Linda Wilson

As time went on with the residents, I introduced seated exercises, and their mobility greatly improved. I even collaborated with a physical therapist I met while visiting one of our residents in the hospital. Networking is essential. I love recycling, so I encouraged family members to bring items like Styrofoam, newspapers, and paper towel rolls for our crafts. I tested each project myself to gauge its difficulty and better assist the residents. A monthly calendar of events was posted, and daily handouts were distributed to residents. We kept the activities and hired entertainment varied to avoid monotony— everything from magicians and singers to grocery store trips and lunch outings.

CHAPTER 22

NAVIGATING GRIEF AND HEALING

It was getting remarkably busy, and I put out the word that I was looking for a volunteer. A wonderful lady by the name of Kathy applied. She was perfect, and little did I know that her husband had recently passed away, which she eventually told me on a very dark day in my life. She mentioned a national group called Grief Share that had meetings every Saturday morning and she invited me to meet the group. Hearing what others are going through will reassure you that your grief is normal. This group was a far cry from the psychologist I saw. Originally, my family doctor sent me to a psychologist, where she wanted me to take more medications. I was currently on an antidepressant and did not want to start taking another pill. The psychologist then sent me to another psychologist. I went one day a week for about a month when I realized I knew more about him than he knew about me. It was time for a drastic change, and I am so happy Kathy introduced me to Grief Share. That was my choice for taking a step that was positive for me.

A Healing Connection: Finding Solace in Grief Share

"Grief Share" is a support group for those who have lost a loved one—whether a parent, spouse, child, friend or even a beloved pet. It is a place where you can speak openly about your emotions, whether you are feeling angry, overwhelmed with sadness, or experiencing the unpredictable highs and lows of grief. These emotions can hit anywhere—at home, at work, in a restaurant, or while shopping. In this space, no one will tell you to 'get over it' or 'stop embarrassing yourself.' There is no set timeline for grieving and no right or wrong way to grieve. Grief is one of the most powerful and personal experiences a person can face. Here, you are free to express your feelings, knowing that healing, though difficult, is a process that takes time."

Things will never be the same, and I know that. I miss him so much, his laugh, his smell, his presence. I sit at the table, and all I see is the EMPTY CHAIR. I can't even see me or anyone else sitting in that EMPTY CHAIR. There is a hole in my heart, in my spirit, that I cannot shake. Some people tell me that I'll get over that in time. That will never happen to me. The only thing I can say is we come into the world with love, and I can say DAVID went out of this world with love. I have never loved anyone or anything in this world more than I love DAVID.

Spending time at Grief Share, I came to realize that I had been suppressing the loss of my baby boy for 59 years. It was not until I began drafting my story that the memory of him surfaced, and with it, the pain of that loss. I often wonder what he would look like now, what kind of relationship we might have had, what vocation he would have chosen, and whether he would have loved me. Perhaps when I leave this earth, I will find the answers to these questions. For now, all I know is that I would love him unconditionally, with all my heart.

CHAPTER 23

WEATHERING THE STORM:

RESILIENCE AND COMMUNITY IN THE WAKE OF HURRICANE IAN

Hurricane Ian battered Florida on September 29, 2022, as a Category 4 storm with maximum sustained winds of around 155 mph. It brought widespread flooding, property damage, and power outages. Even in such difficult times, I am reminded of the resilience of the human spirit and the importance of community. The National Hurricane Center (NHC) warned of severe and life-threatening storm surge inundation of as much as 8 to 10 feet above ground level, with destructive waves ongoing along the southwest coast of Florida.

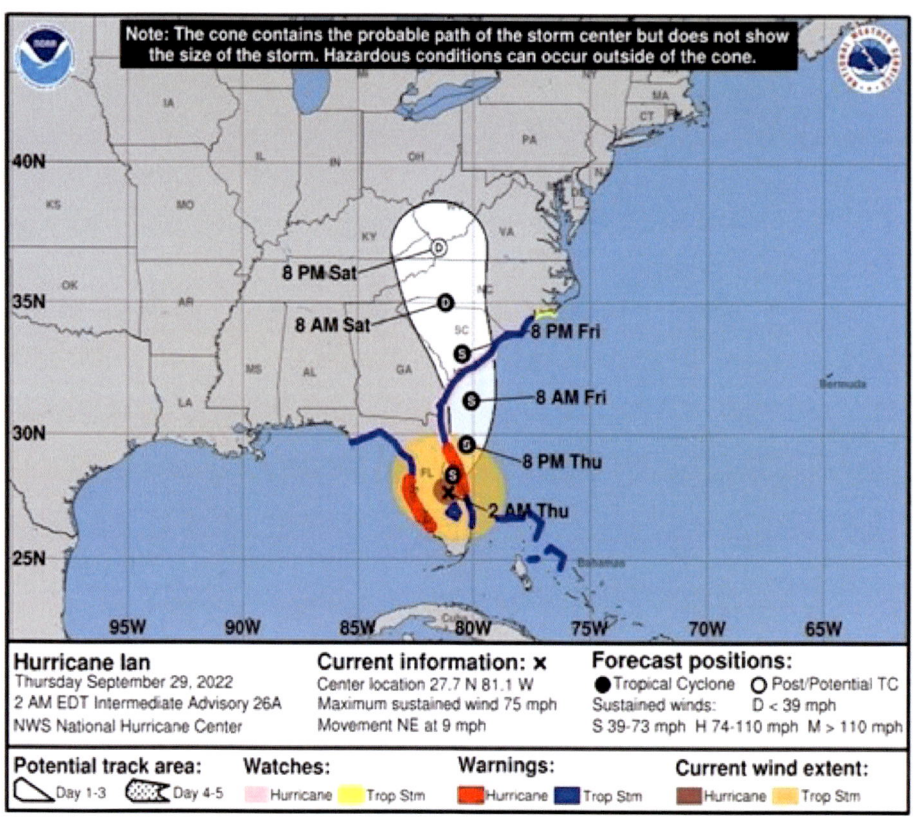

Note: The cone contains the probable path of the storm center but does not show the size of the storm. Hazardous conditions can occur outside of the cone.

Hurricane Ian
Thursday September 29, 2022
2 AM EDT Intermediate Advisory 26A
NWS National Hurricane Center

Current information: x
Center location 27.7 N 81.1 W
Maximum sustained wind 75 mph
Movement NE at 9 mph

Forecast positions:
● Tropical Cyclone ○ Post/Potential TC
Sustained winds: D < 39 mph
S 39-73 mph H 74-110 mph M > 110 mph

Potential track area: ◢ Day 1-3 ⬡ Day 4-5
Watches: ▮ Hurricane ▮ Trop Stm
Warnings: ▮ Hurricane ▮ Trop Stm
Current wind extent: ▮ Hurricane ▮ Trop Stm

Internet Photo

I recall a meeting with the assisted living facility management, and we were told that we could either be a member of Team A or Team B. Team A would stay at the facility until Ian was over, and Team B would be doing the cleanup. I chose to be on Team A and went home, got my sleeping bag, and battened down everything at my home I could. I had activities for the residents, and we did exercises in the hallways while the Hurricane battered our building. Fortunately, our damage was minor compared to our Port Charlotte sister property. It was several months later, and I asked our executive director if we could challenge our sister property to a day of food, beverages, and games. "Great Idea," she said. She will call the executive director in Port Charlotte and arrange the meeting at our facility. I designed games that all residents and staff participate in. I set a date, ordered food, made most of the unique games, and ordered items that would either be worn or made into various activities. It was now less than 4 days away, and I still had no confirmation from Port Charlotte. I have known the executive director of our sister facility, Rebecca since I started running the farmers' market, so I thought it would be OK if I called her since my executive director said she had not heard from her. After reaching her up north, I learned they could not make the original date, so we rescheduled. On the new date, the residents arrived, and we welcomed them with a cheer—the same one I did as a high school cheerleader 61 years ago, though this time seated. Since my executive director was absent, I greeted everyone, outlined the day's activities, and led games like Pool Noodle Golf, tabletop bowling, and a water bucket relay for staff.

For September 2023, we hosted a Great Gatsby dance, with staff and residents dressed in 1920s attire. Music filled the air as staff asked residents, "May I have this dance?"—a phrase that brought back memories. I decorated the second floor in Gatsby style, and we set up a lunch buffet with appetizers, entrées, and desserts. When it came time to award the best-dressed staff and residents, I noticed there were no prizes. My executive director, who had planned the awards, had not mentioned I would need to purchase them. Later, I bought the prizes myself and awarded them, ensuring everyone felt celebrated. From that day on, everything was different. By the end of September, I handed in my letter of resignation to her. She went back to work without saying a word. In October 2023, I came down with Covid. I was ill for about 5 days, and when I recovered, I realized I had lost my sense of taste. It has now been 9 months, and I still cannot taste anything. My time now is spent on cleaning my home, gardening, and drafting my book. I also go to Grief Share, and that has helped me tremendously. Everyone in our group has lost a loved one and understands what each of us is going through.

Sunday Mornings with Friends: Reflections on Life, Aging, and Generations

For over 3 years, I have joined three friends, Kim, Pam, and Audrey, for Sunday morning breakfasts. We chat about community events, recap the past week, and share our health ups and downs. We vent about getting older and wonder how the current generation will navigate a world so different from our own. We have survived WWII, the Great Depression, and the turbulent '60s, and we hope this generation finds its way too. Just as our parents and grandparents once thought we were exhibitionists with our miniskirts, midriff tops, and going braless, we now reflect on the shifts that define each new generation.

CHAPTER 24

MY ROLE AS A MENTOR

I have been blessed in my life with having so many people help me in all my many careers. Now, it is time to give back. I met a young girl who's 25 years old, Lenora, and just starting her career. She is an exceptionally talented artist, and she has recently landed a job as an activity director. As a favor to the executive director, Rebecca, and Chetta, the marketing director, I offered to help Lenora get started. Getting her name and face out to residents at the assisted living facility. Recently, the assisted living facility had some bad press due to the manager, who has now been removed from the organization. The new executive director, Rebecca, has taken on the challenge. Not only hiring new staff members but also refurbishing the building. The Hotel Venice, built in 1926, is a significant historical landmark in Venice, Florida. It was the first building constructed by the Brotherhood of Locomotive Engineers (BLE) as part of their development of the city. Designed in the Northern Italian Renaissance style by architect Leon N. Gillette, the hotel featured 100 luxurious rooms. Notable guests included Thomas Edison, John Ringling, and Ty Cobb. Over the years, the building has served various purposes, including as a winter school for the Kentucky Military Institute from 1932 to 1970. As we are preparing for the 100th Anniversary of the City of Venice, the building is undergoing refurbishment. We have set up an area in the lobby where we are getting the monthly calendar ready. I have shared my contacts in the city, suggested crafts that can be taught to residents, and connected with people who are willing to volunteer their time to help make this community effort.

CHAPTER 25

FINDING YOUR PATH:

BUILDING A LIFE WHEN THE VISION ISN'T CLEAR

Life is like a puzzle and putting it together can seem overwhelming at times. But just like with a puzzle, you start by finding the edges—the foundation. Begin by identifying the key areas of your life that are most important to you, your goals, and what you want to achieve. Break these down into smaller, manageable steps. This approach will help you see progress more clearly and avoid feeling lost in the bigger picture. Teamwork is essential, too; when we are stuck or overwhelmed, letting someone else step in can offer a fresh perspective and relief. Remember, the big picture may be hard to see at first when there are gaps and missing pieces, but as you keep working, the vision becomes clearer. Do not let moments of frustration cause you to give up. Keep pushing forward, even when it feels like the pieces do not fit. Just like I will not let one challenging puzzle defeat me, I encourage you to adopt the same attitude in life. Take time to focus on the details, bit by bit, just as you would with any project or goal. Make room for joy and creativity, find what makes you happy and add more of it to your life. With patience, determination, and the right mindset, the seemingly impossible puzzle of life will come together in ways you never thought possible.

CHAPTER 26

BUILDING LEADERSHIP AND LIFE SKILLS:
A JOURNEY OF GROWTH AND RESPONSIBILITY

Here are some examples of how I accomplished resilience and reinvention in my younger years that carried me through life and can help you accomplish the same. You might call this the border of your "Puzzle Pieces to Life."

A STUDENT COUNCIL MEMBER

Being on the Student Council teaches accountability, as you are entrusted with representing others' interests. This can prepare you for future roles that require trust, dependability, and ethical decision-making.

• **Leadership** – Serving on the Student Council helps you cultivate leadership skills and learn to guide and inspire others, which can be crucial in any future role, whether in your career, community, or personal life.

• **Communication** – You'll develop strong communication abilities by representing your peers, articulating ideas, and discussing important topics, which is valuable in all areas of life.

• **Teamwork** – Student Council emphasizes working collaboratively with others to achieve common goals. This skill is essential in future jobs, family life, or any group endeavor.

• **Problem-Solving** – You'll learn to address issues, make decisions, and find solutions, which prepares you to tackle challenges in life and work.

BEING A CHEERLEADER

Being a cheerleader teaches life lessons that extend far beyond the field or the gym. From teamwork and leadership to discipline and resilience, the skills you learn as a cheerleader prepare you to navigate challenges, inspire others, and pursue success with confidence and determination in any role you take on in life. Here are some key lessons cheerleading imparts:

Teamwork and Collaboration

- Working as a Team: Cheerleading is all about working with others to achieve a common goal. Whether you are performing stunts, coordinating routines, or cheering on the sidelines, you rely on your team, and they rely on you. This teaches you the importance of collaboration and how success is often a group effort.
- Supporting Others: Cheerleaders are literally and figuratively there to lift others up. This spirit of encouragement fosters a mindset of helping others succeed, which is valuable in any personal or professional context.

Leadership and Confidence

- Leading by Example: Cheerleaders are often seen as leaders in their schools or communities. Whether you are leading a cheer, motivating the crowd, or guiding younger members of the squad, you learn how to be a role model and inspire others.
- Building Confidence: Performing in front of large crowds and participating in competitive events builds self-confidence. Cheerleading teaches you to step outside your comfort zone, which can be beneficial in

public speaking, leadership roles, and other areas where confidence is key.

Discipline and Hard Work

- Commitment to Practice: Cheerleading requires dedication, discipline, and regular practice to perfect routines. This instills a strong work ethic and the understanding that success comes through effort and perseverance.
- Time Management: Balancing cheerleading with schoolwork, other activities, and personal life teaches time management skills. This helps later in life when juggling professional responsibilities and personal commitments.

Physical and Mental Toughness

- Physical Strength and Endurance: Cheerleading is physically demanding. It teaches you the importance of taking care of your body, staying fit, and pushing through physical challenges that carry over into maintaining health and well-being later in life.
- Mental Resilience: Cheerleaders often face pressure during performances or competitions, and mistakes happen. Learning to stay calm under pressure, handle mistakes, and bounce back quickly builds mental resilience, which is crucial for facing challenges in life and work.

Communication Skills

- Effective Communication: Cheerleading involves clear, precise communication with teammates, coaches, and sometimes audiences. You learn how to express yourself effectively, give instructions, and collaborate with others in high-pressure environments.

- Listening and Feedback: As part of a team, you learn how to take and give constructive feedback, adjust based on others' input, and communicate openly, all of which are essential in professional environments.

- Handling Criticism and Failure Accepting Criticism: Whether from coaches or judges, cheerleaders receive feedback regularly, both positive and negative. Learning to take criticism constructively helps you improve and builds emotional resilience.

- Overcoming Setbacks: In cheerleading, routines do not always go as planned. Sometimes stunts fail, or performances do not win. Cheerleading teaches you how to handle failure, learn from it, and keep moving forward, which is a critical skill in life.

Positive Attitude and Energy

- Staying Positive: As a cheerleader, one of your main jobs is to stay upbeat and keep the energy high, even when things are not going well for your team. This teaches the power of positivity and how maintaining a good attitude can motivate and inspire others.

- Boosting Morale: Cheerleaders are experts in boosting team spirit, and this translates into adult life in the ability to lift others' spirits, whether in the workplace or personal relationships.

Goal Setting and Achievement

- Working Toward a Goal: Whether it is perfecting a difficult routine or aiming to win a competition, cheerleading involves setting goals and working hard to achieve them. This experience helps develop goal-setting skills that are essential in personal and professional growth.

Public Presence and Presentation Skills

- Performing with Confidence: Cheerleading requires you to perform in front of large audiences, teaching you how to present yourself confidently. This skill can be applied to public speaking, presentations at work, or any situation where you need to command attention and perform under pressure.

- Professionalism: Cheerleaders represent their schools or teams, learning to uphold a standard of professionalism and pride in their role, which translates into maintaining a professional demeanor in the workplace.

- Creative Problem-Solving: From choreographing routines to adapting quickly when stunts or formations do not go as planned, cheerleading encourages creativity and flexibility. Learning to think on your feet and adapt quickly is a valuable skill in many aspects of life.

- Innovation: In cheerleading, you are often encouraged to innovate, whether through new routines or creative cheers. This fosters a mindset of continuous improvement and innovation, which can be applied in careers and personal development.

BENEFITS OF JOINING A HIGH SCHOOL OR COLLEGE SORORITY

Joining a sorority in high school or college can enhance your high school or college experience, offering a balance of social connection, personal development, and the chance to make a positive impact in your community. Building Strong Friendships – A sorority provides an immediate support system and a group of peers who often share similar interests and values. It can help you form lifelong friendships and create a sense of belonging.

Developing Leadership Skills

- Sororities often involve organizational responsibilities, event planning, and community service projects, which give you a chance to develop leadership and teamwork skills early on.

Giving Back to the Community

- Many sororities have a focus on philanthropy and community service, allowing you to contribute to meaningful causes and develop a sense of civic responsibility.

Expanding Social Skills

- Through regular meetings, events, and activities, sorority life encourages you to communicate effectively, meet new people, and learn how to build positive relationships.

Creating Lasting Memories

- From group activities to school events, being part of a sorority allows you to make memories and experiences that are unique to your high school or college years.

Networking Opportunities

- Being part of a sorority connects you with members from other schools, alumni, and community leaders, which can provide valuable support and mentorship both in high school and beyond.

CHAPTER 27

FACING MOTHER NATURES WRATH

Experiencing a hurricane, avalanche, fire, or flood at a young age teaches valuable life lessons in resilience, adaptability, teamwork, and emotional strength. With proper support, young people can emerge from the experience stronger, more empathetic, and better equipped to handle future challenges.

Resilience and Adaptability

- Facing Uncertainty: Experiencing the chaos of a natural disaster teaches young people how to cope with uncertainty and unexpected challenges. It shows them that life can change quickly, and they may learn to adapt to difficult or even dangerous situations.

- Emotional Strength: Surviving a hurricane or flood can foster resilience. While it may bring fear, anxiety, and stress, overcoming such a traumatic event helps children and young adults realize their own inner strength and ability to persevere through tough times.

Appreciation for Safety and Security

- Value of Stability: Living through the instability and destruction caused by a hurricane, fire, or flood can make young people appreciate the stability of everyday life. It underscores the importance of having a safe place to live, access to necessities, and a sense of normalcy.

- Gratitude for Essentials: They may become more aware of the basic things in life—like clean water, electricity, and shelter—which are easy to take for granted until they are lost during a disaster.

The Power of Community and Teamwork

- Sense of Togetherness: Natural disasters often bring communities together. Young people see firsthand how neighbors, friends, and strangers come together to help one another. This can instill the importance of teamwork, mutual support, and the strength of community in difficult times.

- Many kids and teens are involved in cleanup efforts or volunteer with their families to assist others affected by the disaster. This teaches them the importance of compassion, empathy, and taking action to support those in need.

Learning to Prepare and Plan

- Preparedness: Going through a hurricane, fire, or flood teaches the importance of preparation. Children and teens may learn about emergency planning, such as gathering supplies, following evacuation orders, and knowing what to do when disaster strikes.

- These skills can shape their sense of responsibility and foresight later in life.

- Problem-Solving Under Pressure: Being in a crisis can help young people develop problem-solving skills. They learn how to stay calm, make decisions under pressure, and think creatively when normal resources or routines are disrupted.

Coping with Fear and Trauma

- Managing Emotions: Hurricanes. Fire and floods are scary experiences, especially for young people. They often feel powerless in the face of nature's forces. These events can teach children how to cope with fear and anxiety, particularly with the support of family and community.

- Emotional Growth: The experience of losing possessions, seeing damage, or even the possibility of danger can be traumatic, but with support, young people can learn to process these emotions and grow emotionally from the experience.

Environmental Awareness

- Understanding Nature's Power: Going through a natural disaster often increases a young person's respect for nature and its forces. They may become more aware of the environment and how natural events like hurricanes and floods affect people, ecosystems, and the planet.

- Climate Awareness: Older children and teens may begin to connect these events with larger issues like climate change or the importance of environmental conservation, leading to a sense of responsibility for the future.

Overall, Lessons:

- Overcoming Adversity: A hurricane or flood can teach young people how to recover from hardship, how to rebuild after loss, and how to approach future challenges with courage and hope.

- Empathy and Compassion: Witnessing the struggles of others and being part of a community response can develop a greater sense of empathy, compassion, and the desire to help others.

- Resilience in the Face of Uncertainty: These experiences can build lifelong resilience, teaching young people that even in the face of disaster, they have the strength and resources to persevere and eventually find stability again.

CHAPTER 28

THE FINAL PIECE: PUTTING IT ALL TOGETHER

My story may have begun long ago, perhaps before some of you were even born. You may not have experienced divorce, floods, hurricanes, tornadoes, riots, avalanches, the loss of a child, or the loss of a great love. But life will present its own set of challenges, and you have the power to make your life the best it can be.

When it comes to choosing a vocation, ask yourself: What do I love to do? What interests me? Pursue your dreams. This is something only you can control. If it is financial resources you need, find a job and save. If there is someone you admire, ask if they would mentor you. Look into local organizations that offer grants. If you are in the military, reach out to programs like your VA Transition Assistance Program (TAP). About 200,000 Service members transition to civilian life each year. The Transition Assistance Program (TAP) provides information, resources, and tools to Service members and their loved ones to help prepare for the move from military to civilian life. Service members begin TAP one year prior to separation or two years prior to retiring. Reach out to your church, community centers, or any support system available.

You do not necessarily need a college degree to succeed in life today. You can be anything you want to be. But having a degree can certainly help, especially in fields like medicine or law. The world has so much to offer you, and you can achieve anything you set your mind to. If you can imagine it, you can do it—by taking action!

I will not pretend it will be easy. As you already know, life is full of OPPORTUNITIES, TIMING, NETWORKING, CHOICES, and HARDWORK.. And it is you, and only you, who can turn your dreams into reality. One of the cornerstones of life is the power of choice. Remember, you cannot always expect to receive what you give, but that should not stop you from giving your best.

One day, you will tell your own story of how you overcame the challenges you faced. That story will become someone else's survival guide. Life is never complete and is constantly in flux. It requires compromise, hard work, and honest conversations.

Why this story – why now?

Because women's stories – especially those built on courage rather than credentials- are essential. Resilience is not linear and every underdog deserves their original story. This is about a woman's life, lived on her own terms, and changing hearts.

LIFE'S'PUZZLE PIECES – MY STORY OF RESILIENCE AND REINVENTION – HOW YOU CAN ACHIEVE IT TOO is a deeply human, unique story. It is for every person who ever asked, "What if I'm not enough?" and went on to prove that they were. This is not just a book. It is a message. You are actively shaping your reality, whether you realize it or not. Life itself is not easy, but if you can imagine it, then you must take action to bring it to life. So, instead of saying "THE END," I will leave you with this:

IMAGINE-ACTION

HELPFUL LANGUAGE TIPS FOR YOUNG AND OLD

Language evolves with time, and many terms have been replaced by newer, more contemporary words or phrases. Here are some examples of how language has shifted over recent decades:

Job Terminology

- Part-time job   Gig
- Permanent job   Full-time position
- Temp   Freelancer/Contractor
- Side job   Side hustle

Technology and Communication

- Electronic mail   Email
- Surfing the internet   Browsing/Scrolling
- World Wide Web   The internet/Web
- Chat room   Online Community/Forum
- Long-distance call   Video call/Zoom call

Lifestyle and Social Trends

- Second-hand store   Thrift shop/Resale boutique
- Youth subculture   Tribe/Community
- Junk food   Fast food
- Health food store   Whole foods market/Natural grocer
- Fitness center   Gym/Wellness center

Business and Economy

- Start-up company   Entrepreneurial venture/Start-up
- Mom-and-pop store   Small business/Local shop
- Work from home   Remote work/Telecommuting/WFH
- Multinational company   Global enterprise
- Networking event   Meet-up/Networking session

Education and Learning

- Distance learning   Online learning/E-learning
- Continuing education   Professional development/Lifelong learning
- Correspondence course   Online course/Remote learning
- Extracurricular activities   Enrichment programs

Entertainment and Media

- Record album   Vinyl/LP
- Movie theater   Cinema
- Home video   Streaming/On-demand
- Television show   TV series/Streaming series

Social and Cultural Concepts

- Social network   Social media platform
- Pen pal   Online friend/Virtual friend
- Boyfriend/Girlfriend   Partner/Significant other
- Environmental movement   Sustainability/Climate action

Technology and Gadgets

- Mobile phone   Smartphone
- Pager   Messaging app/Instant messenger
- Personal computer (PC)   Laptop/Desktop
- Game console   Gaming system

Consumer and Retail

- Catalog shopping   Online shopping/E-commerce
- Department store   Big-box store/Retail giant
- Sale   Discount event/Flash sale
- Woodstock hippie vibes   Boho Chic

Health and Wellness

- Physical fitness   Wellness/Personal Fitness
- Mental health care   Mindfulness/Well-being
- Dieting   Healthy eating/Lifestyle change

These changes reflect shifts in society, culture, technology, and communication styles. The newer terms often reflect more modern or nuanced understandings of the concepts they describe.

ACKNOWLEDGEMENTS

A heartfelt thank you to Kim Cool, whose insight finally led me to explore and share my story. She asked me, "How did you lay your path to so many different careers without a college education and still find success?" It was a question I had heard many times as I grew older, but when I started asking it of myself, I could finally see how the puzzle pieces of my life came together perfectly. This book is a tribute to all of you who asked that question and encouraged me to find the answer.

BIBLIOGRAPHY

PERIODICALS

- "The Joplin Globe."
- "Flood of 1955" Published by John F. Caputi
- "Western Connecticut's Great Flood Disaster" Published by The Waterbury
- (Conn.) Republican-American
- "The Torrington Register"
- "Hartford Courant" Published on 2/9/1998.
- "Sarasota Herald-Tribune" Published on 5/12/2003.

BOOKS:

- "The New Farmers' Market" By Vence Corum, Marcie Rosenzweig and Eric Gibson
- BC Brunswick - Defense Group, Technical Products Division, Skokie, Illinois

WEBSITES:

- **https://en.wikipedia.org/wiki/Scan-Optics**

- **https://www.wyssenavalanche.com/en/**

  - w.skiutah.com/blog/authors/lexi/last-gunners-the-conclusion-of-alta1
  - https://www.sap.com/about/what-is-sap.html#what-does-sap-do
  - https://benefits.va.gov/transition/tap.asp
  - https://www.bing.com/images/search? Alligator Alley

- https://www.bing.com/images/search?view=detailV2&ccid=f6VqaHB6&id=F3AEE128945586D2 8776D

- https://www.bing.com/images/search?q=maps+of+florida&qs=n&form=QBILPG&sp=-1&ghc=1&lq=0&pq=maps+of+florida&sc=10-15&cvid=34078AE07C4342F7B74C1EC617895E4A&ghsh=0&ghacc=0&first=1

- Historic Asolo Theater, Sarasota | cityseeker

- https://www.investopedia.com/terms/i/international-organization-for-standardization-iso.aspbig household.

- https://en.wikipedia.org/wiki/Total_quality_management

"SOURCE NOTES"

- "Some of the information referenced in this book was drawn from various internet articles, booklets, and other sources such as grief and mental health."

RECOGNITION IN AWARDS-CERTIFICATES-EDUCATION

YEAR   AWARD-CERTIFICATES-EDUCATION

04/07/1959 THE DAUGHTERS OF THE AMERICAN REVOLUTION

1961	DIPLOMA FOWLER SCHOOL
1963 and 1964	ANSONIA HIGH SCHOOL STUDENT COUNCIL
06/07/1984	TELESIS SYSTEMS CORP. TRAINING PROGRAM
01/22/1991	VIDEO SCRIPTWRITING COURSE
01/06/1992	PROGRESSIVE MANAGEMENT ASSOC. – LEADEREFFTIVENESS TRANING
09/09/1994	PLASTICS DESIGN FORUM (2 CEUs)
03/15/1997	TOTAL QUALITY MANAGEMENT TRAINING – DAVIS LEARNING RESOURCES AND THE CONNECTICUT QUALITY COUNCIL
04/02/1997	WORCESTER POLYTECHNIC INSTITUTE (WPI) QUALITY IMPROVEMENT CERTIFICATE PROGRAM
06/12/1998	CONNECTICUT AWARD FOR EXCELLENCE – NUTMEG AWARD
03/15/1999	SAP TRAINING & EDUCATION CERTIFICATE
09/20/2011	VENICE AREA CHAMBER OF COMMERCE – AMBASSADORS COUNCIL CELEBRATION

11/07/2011	AMERICAN FARMLAND TRUST FAVORITE FARMER'S MARKET
YEAR AWARD/CERTIFICATES/EDUCATION	
11/07/2011	AMERICAN FARMLAND TRUST FAVORITE FARMER'S MARKET IN THE STATE OF FLORIDA
09/26/2013	FLORIDA POLICE ACCREDITATION COALITION, INC
05/09/2014	CITIZENS POLICE ACADEMY
12/08/2014	VENICE MAINSTREET - DONATIONS AWARD
05/11/2017	VISIT SARASOTA COUNTY - 2017 NATIONAL TRAVEL & TOURISM WEEK CATEGORY: MANAGEMENT- 1ST PLACE OUT OF 12 NOMINEES
12/30/2017	CERTIFICATE OF APPRECIATION - VOLUNTEER FROM VENICE POLICE DEPARTMENT
12/30/2019	CERTIFICATE OF APPRECIATION - INVOLVING VOLUNTEER SERVICES
06/27/2020	CERTIFICATE OF APPRECIATION – VOLUNTEER PERFORMING COMPREHENSIVE INVENTORY AND LOGICAL ITEMS DISPOSAL PROCESS IN VPD PROPERTY & EVIDENCE DEPT.
06/27/2020	CIVILIANCITATON AWARD – APPREHENSION OF A DANGEROUS CRIMINAL
04-26-2025	MICHIGAN STATE UNIVERSITY COURSERA CERTIFICATE IN SCRIPT WRITING